# Situating Caribbean Literature and Criticism in Multicultural and Postcolonial Studies

Tamara Alvarez-Detrell and Michael G. Paulson
*General Editors*

Vol. 11

PETER LANG
New York • Washington, D.C./Baltimore • Bern
Frankfurt am Main • Berlin • Brussels • Vienna • Oxford

Seodial Frank H. Deena

# Situating Caribbean Literature and Criticism in Multicultural and Postcolonial Studies

PETER LANG
New York • Washington, D.C./Baltimore • Bern
Frankfurt am Main • Berlin • Brussels • Vienna • Oxford

Library of Congress Cataloging-in-Publication Data

Deena, Seodial Frank H.
Situating Caribbean literature and criticism in multicultural and postcolonial studies /
Seodial Frank H. Deena.
p. cm. — (Caribbean studies; vol. 11)
Includes bibliographical references and index.
1. Caribbean literature—21st century—History and criticism.
PN849.C3 D43    809'.897290905—dc22    2008006211
ISBN 978-0-8204-6222-6
ISSN 1098-4186


Bibliographic information published by **Die Deutsche Bibliothek**.
**Die Deutsche Bibliothek** lists this publication in the "Deutsche
Nationalbibliografie"; detailed bibliographic data is available
on the Internet at http://dnb.ddb.de/.

The paper in this book meets the guidelines for permanence and durability
of the Committee on Production Guidelines for Book Longevity
of the Council of Library Resources.

© 2009 Peter Lang Publishing, Inc., New York
29 Broadway, 18th floor, New York, NY 10006
www.peterlang.com

Printed in the United States of America

# Contents

# Acknowledgments

I wish to thank the Thomas Harriot College of Arts and Sciences of East Carolina University for excellent support and Ms. Jackie Pavlovic from Peter Lang for her patience and fine production work. Teresa Howell, my Graduate Assistant, has worked sacrificially on the editing and camera-readying of this work. Special gratitude to my family and friends—especially my wife, Debbie, children, Shivaun, Esther, Rachel, and David, and mother-in-law, Winifred Morris. I dedicate this book to my friend, O. R. Dathorne (1934-2007), my niece Lorna (Nadia) Ramsarran (1974-2008), and my daughter Shivaun during her time of recovery.

Special thanks to Peter Lang Publishing, Inc. and the editor of *Journal of Caribbean Studies* for publishing sections of chapters and for permission to use these sections: "Disorder and Mimicry through Colonial Apparatuses in V. S. Naipaul's *The Mimic Men*," and "Colonial Alienation Producing Madness in Jean Rhys' *Wide Sargasso Sea*," from *Canonization, Colonization, Decolonization: A Comparative Study of Political and Critical Works by Minority Writers*. New York: Peter Lang Publishing Inc., 2001, pages 71-91 and 91-119, respectively and "A Critical Overview of Caribbean Studies as Pioneer of and Central to Postcolonial and Multicultural Studies." *Journal of Caribbean Studies* 22.3 (Spring 2008): 215-30, "Color Complication and Confrontation in Caribbean Culture as Depicted in Trevor Rhone's *Old Story Time*." *Journal of Caribbean Studies* 20.3 (Spring 2006): 219-27, and "Multicultural and Postcolonial Interpretations of Caribbean Literature and Its Environment." *Journal of Caribbean Studies* 18.3 (Fall 2004): 163-82.

# A Critical Overview of Caribbean Literature

Through its marriage with postcolonial and multicultural studies, Caribbean Criticism has become an emergent and a popular culture–producing Twenty-First Century cutting-edge literature and two Nobel Literature Laureates–Derek Walcott (1992) and V. S. Naipaul (2001). The Caribbean, however, more than any other region, has suffered most uniquely from colonial exploitation, oppression, and marginalization; but it is only now receiving some critical attention and international recognition. Proportionately, in geography and population, to other regions like India, Africa, and Central and South America, the Caribbean or West Indies has been the recipient of a longer and more intense period of colonial domination and fragmentation. The eye of the hurricane–Hurricane European Colonization (HEC)–has hit the innocent and unprepared Caribbean in a ferocious and devastating manner. Bill Ashcroft, Gareth Griffiths, and Helen Tiffin concur, in *The Empire Writes Back* that, "in the Caribbean, the European imperial enterprise ensured that the worst features of colonialism throughout the globe would all be combined in one region" (145). In reality, slavery in the Caribbean commenced from the time of Christopher Columbus' discovery or rediscovery of Hispaniola in 1492, and ceased in the 1960s, which means over 550 years of displacement and dislocation.

Prior to Columbus' entrance in the Caribbean, Amerindians occupied all the Caribbean Islands, and these inhabitants were the center of Caribbean life, culture, and history. But European's entrance and presence in the Caribbean forced a massive and most cruel genocide of the natives. "Virtually eliminated," except for a small percentage in Dominica and Guyana, the inhabitants of the Caribbean found themselves pushed from the center of life, culture, and history through oppression and exploitation from the colonizer. This sociological picture of marginalization parallels the Natives' marginalization in Caribbean literature:

> ...the aboriginal Indian seldom appears, and is not a centre of social and political interest either in verse, in drama, or in fiction by writers from the West Indies, indeed, the fiction in which the contemporary Indians do appear either registers them as detribalised individuals in the towns ("Bucks") or portrays them as exotic groups in the interior. (Ramchand 51)

Few writers—H. G. deLister, Edgar Mittleholzer, Wilson Harris, Jan Crew, and Derek Walcott—include the Amerindian presence in their works, but apart from Wilson Harris, the other writers place the natives outside the center of action; as background, foil characters, or props. Wilson Harris, however, "discovers relevance in the Indians, involving them in three of the basic themes of his fiction: the unity of all men, the theme of rebirth, and the search for ancestral roots" (Ramchand 51).

## Slavery

According to Colin A. Palmer, the Amerindians were "enslaved and required to work in the fields, households, and mines. But many Indians soon died from mistreatment and disease, which created a shortage of labor" (8). After several years of death, disease, and genocide, the drastic demise of the Indian population provided the opportunity for the Spanish to request African slaves in 1501—capitalizing on the 1479 Treaty that Portugal had agreed to supply the Spanish with African slaves, and by 1502 the machinery of the Slave Trade to the Caribbean began (7-9). By 1650, the Dutch, French, and English joined the Portuguese and Spanish in their "human commerce" (10). Through the Atlantic Slave Trade between 1502 and 1870, 10 to 12 million slaves were imported to the Americas and Caribbean. From this conservative figure, 0.2 million went to Central America, 0.5 million to South America, 0.5 million to the United States of America, 5 million to Brazil, and 5 million to the Caribbean. The Caribbean alone had 42% of African slaves, and with neighboring Brazil they had 84% of the African slaves (Palmer 8-20).

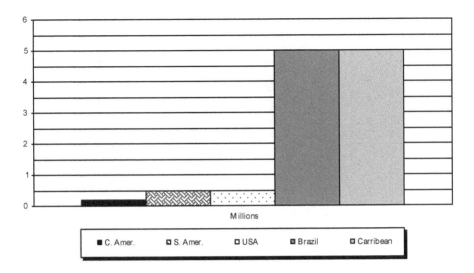

Figure 1: The Atlantic Slave Trade

# Indentureship

Slavery in the Caribbean was succeeded by Indian indentureship during the period of 1838-1917. According to Moses Seenarine:

> From the 1500s onwards, European settlers colonized the Caribbean and Americas with enslaved Africans and indentured Indians and other ethnic groups who worked on their plantations. These capitalists needed labor to generate profits and so indenture, like slavery, became from the start, a violent, involuntary process in which hundreds of thousands of people were kidnapped and tricked into migrating from South Asia. Many Indian families today tell a common tale of how their ancestors explain they were tricked into migrating. Due to a shortage, women were exploited the most and many were abused then compelled to migrate; at the Depot, girls and women were often separated from their families to fill up a ship's quotas; and so on. (Foreword)

But this was part of a larger indentureship, the third wave of Indian migration, according to Mahin Gosine:

> East Indian movement out of India during the indentureship period was rather profound as millions began settling in numerous countries around the world. The indenture system was introduced in Nigeria, for example, in 1834, in Uganda in 1834, in Mauritius in 1834, in Guyana in 1838, in New Zealand in 1840, in Trinidad in 1845, in Suriname in 1873, and in Fiji in 1879. Most of these countries received significant numbers of indentured East Indian laborers (Motwani, 1989). During the

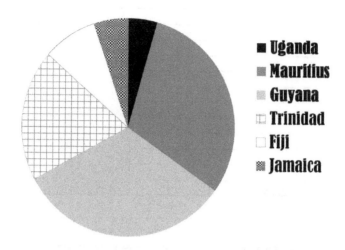

**Figure 2: Comparative View of Indentured Laborers**

indentureship period, Uganda received 32,000 East Indians, Mauritius 225,000, Guyana 239,000, Trinidad 144,000, and Fiji 61,000. Smaller numbers of East Indian indentured laborers were also transported to such countries as Jamaica, St. Lucia, Guadeloupe, Grenada, Hawaii, and a few others. Jamaica, for example, received 39,000 East Indians between 1845 and 1917, the duration of the indenture system in that country. Grenada received 5,000 East Indian indentured workers, Guadeloupe 22,000, and St. Lucia 2,000. The indenture system was halted in 1917 in most of the receiving societies around the world. (Sojourner to Settler: An Introduction)

In totality, European imperialism in the Caribbean resulted in "the virtual annihilation of the native population of Caribs and Arawaks, the plundering and internecine piracy amongst the European powers, the deracination and atrocities of the slave trade and plantation slavery, the subsequent systems of indenture which 'stranded' Chinese and Indians in the Caribbean when the return clause of indenture contracts were dishonored" (Ashcroft, Griffiths, and Tiffin, *Empire*, 145–46).

## Silencing

In an era of globalization, the Caribbean continues to experience neo-colonial silencing and domination. It is too small, too poor, and too fragmented, some would claim, to be a major player in the world of international politics, economics, and culture, thus, leaving West Indians with the alternatives of mimicry (Naipaul's *The Mimic Men*), madness (Rhys' *Wide Sargasso Sea*), and migration (Lamming's *In the Castle of My Skin*, Naipaul's *Miguel Street*, Selvon's *The Lonely Londoners*). This region—rich in natural, tourist, and manufacturing resources—has supplied several European nations with wealth and intellect to expand their Empires. It has also supplied the luxury and culture to refresh and refurbish millions of diseased and decaying tourist and business enterprises. Yet, the Caribbean has never been the host of World Cup Soccer, Olympics, and International Conferences. For the first time in its history, World Cup Cricket was played in the Caribbean in 2007, even though the West Indies won the historic first World Cup Cricket in 1976. In the recent documentary series, *End of Empire*, produced by Brian Lapping, the only region that was not produced was the Caribbean. Lack of finance was cited as the reason for this omission. The recent Oxford University Press' five-volume history of the British Empire, not only failed to discuss the Caribbean in a reasonable manner, but also failed to seek insights from the West Indian historians (Louis). Even as late as the turn of the twentieth century—which witnessed major historical changes as emancipation of slavery, dismantling of indentureship and apartheid, granting of voting rights to African Americans and women in America, and the toppling of dictators' regimes—the history of the British Empire, which includes more than two thirds of the world, was written from new imperialist perspective. Domination, though, continues in the Caribbean in a subtle, neocolonial form, as well as in overt and visible manner such as the 1986 US invasion of the tiny Grenada.

Through the analysis of works and reference by Frantz Fanon, Derek Walcott, Edward Glissant, Jean Rhys, V. S. Naipaul, George Lamming, E. R. Brathwaite, Zee Edgell, Earl Lovelace, Trevor Rhone, Mere Collins, Samuel Selvon, Michelle Cliff, Jamaica Kincaid, Esmeralda Santiago, Wilson Harris, and Caryl Phillips, this book explores Caribbean studies as pioneer of and central to postcolonial and multicultural studies. This chapter provides a brief critical overview of Caribbean Literature.

## Aftermath

The twentieth century will be documented as one of the greatest centuries witnessing the confrontation of the aftermath of the abolition of slavery, cessation of indentureship, end of the British Empire and colonization, expansion of the traditional literary canon, the granting of voting rights to women and African Americans, the re-emergence of feminism, postcolonialism, multiculturalism, and globalization. Yet in 1992, when Nobel literature laureate, Derek Walcott, from the small Caribbean island of St. Lucia, received the Nobel Prize in Literature, the world was still plagued by wars and conflicts on the bases of race, class, gender, religion, education, and politics. Many regions and nations were still partitioned and dehumanized. Wars in Serbia, Africa, Central America, and the Mideast raged viciously, ravishing human lives and dignity. Against this background, the leading Caribbean playwright and poet stepped up to the podium to receive his prize, but also to deliver a powerful and revolutionary message to the rest of the world, especially Europe. "The history of the world," points out Walcott, "by which of course we mean Europe, is a record of intertribal lacerations, of ethnic cleansings," (Nobel Lecture 30). In 2001, when V. S. Naipaul won the Nobel Prize for Literature, the world plunged deeper into the throes of violence, hate, and destruction. Terrorism grabbed the world's attention, both globally and personally, dramatically and violently. The destruction of the World Trade Center (lives of human beings from hundreds of nations) symbolized intentions to fragment and crush international, intercultural, and interdisciplinary global unity and order, but, at the same time, it further reinforced the importance of multicultural and postcolonial studies. Racial, ethnic, religious, cultural, and tribal conflicts continue to impregnate hate crimes, suicide bombing, ethnic cleansing, arms race for mass destruction, intolerance and bigotry, and spiritual and psychological enslavement. Naipaul used his own struggle to internationalize his world as a message against the attacks of the globalization and diversification of the world: "So as a child I had this sense of two worlds, the world outside that tall corrugated-iron gate, and the world at home—or, at any rate, the world of my grandmother's house. It was a remnant of our caste sense, the thing that excluded and shut out" (Nobel Lecture). His pursuit of a wider, more integrated world was realized in Trinidad, and later in England as he traveled and wrote:

> Away from this world of my grandmother's house, where we ate rice in the middle of the day and wheat in the evenings, there was the great unknown—in this island of only 400,000 people. There were the African or African-derived people who were the majority....There were the white people, not all of them English; and the Portuguese and the Chinese, at one time also immigrants like us. And, more mysterious than these, were the people we called Spanish, 'pagnols, mixed people of warm brown complexions who came from the Spanish time, before the island was detached from Venezuela and the Spanish Empire—a kind of history absolutely beyond my child's comprehension. (Nobel Lecture)

Books and travels aided Naipaul's quest for knowledge and understanding of his Indian and Caribbean world, then African, South American, and Muslim Worlds. His aim was always to fill out his world picture (Nobel Lecture). Like Walcott and Naipaul, many other Caribbean writers like Wilson Harris, Michelle Cliff, George Lamming, Erna Brodber, and Fantz Fanon have been Sounding the trumpet for national, regional, and international integration and promotion.

## Regionalism

A significant attempt and pioneering thrust placed nationalism and regionalism at the center of a "spirited debate" (Katizinski 139), with the launching of several Caribbean literary journals in the 1940s, including Frank Collymore's *Bim* (Barbados 1942), Edna Manley's *Focus* (Jamaica 1943), Arthur J. Seymour's *Kyk-over-al* (Guyana 1945), Aime Cesaire's *Tropiques* (Martinique 1941), and UWI's *Caribbean Quarterly* (1949). *Casa delas Americas* was added after Cuba's revolution, and thereafter *Journal of Caribbean Studies*, *Journal of West Indian Literature*, *Callaloo*, *Commonwealth Review*, *Commonwealth Novel in English*, *Griot*, and *Ariel*. Several associations like Association of Caribbean Studies, International Conference on Caribbean Literature, Caribbean Association Studies, and West Indian Literature Association were also founded.

In the late 1960s as Caribbean Literature sought to establish itself in the Caribbean, England, and later in North America, several prominent literary critics warned West Indian writers and the literary community about the "dangers inherent in allowing external perceptions to dominate the evaluation of West Indian literature" (Allis 23). The greatest danger rested on the fact that the colonizer-colonized relationship dictated the relationship between British critics and West Indian writers. These critics became "patronizing and simplistic" towards the writers (26), but the imperialist agenda almost succeeded in crippling Caribbean literature. Allis further illustrates how "British critics writing in the popular press—The *London Times*, *London Sunday Observer*, *Times Literary Supplement*, *New Statesman*, *Spectator*, and *Listener*—approached this new literature from a similarly benign point of view" (26). British reviews and criticism viciously attacked Caribbean writers' language, style, content, characterization, and even their presence in London.

A pattern of British hostility found continuation in North American criticism. Caribbean literature came to the United States of America from London, and white American reviews of the fifties and sixties "showed a tendency

to regard West Indian writers as naive and incapable of grasping the significance of their subject matter" (Allis 31). African American reviews initially attacked Caribbean writers on the basis of racial alliance. A 1972 review in
*Freedomways* notes that Lamming's *"Natives of My Person* is rendered in a language and style that are simply too European to excite the interest of readers
who are pretty turned-off by the symbols of white culture" (qtd. in Allis 34).
Both British and American critics operated in a highly neocolonialist manner
towards Caribbean Literature:

> These colonial critics, described by Jomo Kenyatta as "professional friends and
> interpreters of the African" are people who acquire a most proprietorial air when
> talking of the part of Africa they have happened to visit; they carve a personal sphere
> of influence and champion the most reactionary and the most separatist cause of
> whichever group among whom they happen to live. They are again most vehement in
> pointing out the unique intelligence, amiability and quick will of their adopted areas
> and groups. (Ngugi, *Homecoming* xviii-xix)

In reality, Caribbean writers and critics have been swimming against the tides
of slavery and colonization aftermath. Antonio Benitez Rojo asks, "how can
one even begin to talk about Caribbean literature when its very existence is in
question?" (xxx-xxxi). C. L. R. James and V. S. Naipaul (Trinidad), Alejo
Carpentier and Roberto Fernandez (Cuba), Aime Cesaire, and Edward
Glissant (Martinique), Edward Kamau Brathwaite and George Lamming
(Barbados), Derek Walcott (St. Lucia), Claude McKay and Michelle Cliff
(Jamaica), Jamaica Kincaid (Antigua), and Wilson Harris and Walter Rodney
(Guyana) have been pulling down colonial mythic walls of Caribbean culture
and rebuilding Caribbean reality.

## Discovery and Definition

Calls for "deracialization of all cultural claims began with Fanon," and
have since been repeated by Walcott, Lamming, and Brathwaite; and elaborated by Glissant and Guyanese 1987 literary laureate, Wilson Harris (Katzinski 140). In "Caribbean Critics" (1969), Brathwaite defends the idea of a
Caribbean culture "different from, though not exclusive of Europe" that exists
as a "complex of voices and patterns held together by geography, political force
and social interaction" (*Roots* 114). His Pan Africanism informed, since his return from Ghana in 1963, *Arrivants* trilogy (1973), "The African Presence in
the Caribbean" (1974), and *History of the Voice* (1984). Through the influence
of African and African American focus on centering Africa in the cultural and
educational studies of people of African linkages across the world, the Black

Power Movement along with Black Theology reached the islands in the late 1960s. Molefi Asante popularized Afrocentrism in the United States of America, while historian and social theorist C. L. R. James shared the Afrocentric Idea in the Caribbean with Brathwaite. James' "From Toussaint L'Ouverture to Fidel Castro" (1963) advanced the argument, but Walcott rejects the idea that postcoloniality is in Garveyism—back to Africa movement. Walcott argued that the real enemy of the "colonial artist was not the people, or the people's crude aesthetic which he refined and orchestrated, but those who had elected themselves as protectors of the people, frauds who cried out against indignities done to the people, who urged them to acquire pride which meant abandoning their individual dignity, who cried out that black was beautiful like transmitters from a different revolution without explaining what they meant by beauty" (Walcott, "Twilight" 35). This post independence elite, for Walcott, becomes the new hirelings, who, with their "rough philosophies," were recalling the "old devils to political use. Witch doctors of the new left with imported totems," who were already "exorcised" by an older world. This was the new post independent betrayal (Walcott, "Twilight" 35).

Michael Dash's translation of Glissant's *Caribbean Discourse* (1989) suggests "affinities between Glissant's notion of metissage (synchronic relations within and across cultures) and antillanite and Harris' ongoing re-visions of Caribbean and New World identities" from *Tradition, the Writer and Society* (1967) and *Explorations* (1981) to *The Womb of Space: The Cross-Cultural Imagination* (1967) (Katzinski 140). The starting point of both Glissant and Harris is the "demythification of the self and the emphasis on the structuring potential of the collective unconscious" (Katzinski 140). Harris writes that the remarkableness of the West Indian "is a sense of subtle links, the series of subtle and nebulous links which are latent within him, the latent ground of all old and new personalities" (*Tradition* 28). What is the Caribbean? Glissant asks, simultaneously, other than "a multiple series of relationships" (*Caribbean* 139). Walcott believes that postcolonial writers and critics are like the second Adam to restore, rename, and redeem (*Another Life* 145). Influenced by Fanon's critique of Negritude in *Black Skin, White Mask* (1952) and *The Wretched of the Earth* (1962), the 1992 Nobel literature laureate's works and his Nobel speech have urged the world to look on the Caribbean as "a house on the side of a country road ... whose smell is the smell of refreshing possibility as well as survival" ("Nobel Lecture" 30). He uses the postcolonial and multicultural Caribbean as the brazen serpent of healing and restoration for a world plagued by racial and cultural lacerations ("Nobel Lecture" 31). The Caribbean, therefore, becomes a bridge over troubled waters because it is like "the glue ... the love that reassembles our African and Asiatic fragments" (28). It is this diverse richness that

10

ɔn sense and simplicity of the ordinary West Indians, as repre-
an, who are successful in ideological and practical decoloniza-
:olonialism, these important voices from the Caribbean—and
otʜ. colonies—were silenced, but in a global and postcolonial era,
these voices are paving the way to replace the old colonial system of brute,
force, and ignorance allowing homogeneity—with the new global and multicultural system of dialogue, understanding, and knowledge allowing heterogeneity for respect and democracy of all peoples.

## Complications

The Caribbean socio-economic, historical, and political past complicates its
"fabric of divisions and diversities" (Bhatnager 30). Because of its mixture of
people from Africa, India, and Europe, there is a uniquely diverse
composition of personalities and approaches. Dolly Zulakha Hassan describes
the West Indian society as one "made up of different peoples—an amalgam of
Whites, Blacks, East Indians, Chinese, Portuguese, mixed races, and in
Jamaica, Jews and Lebanese—uprooted and displaced from their original
cultures" (4). Naipaul uses a universal approach to correct and rebuild the
Caribbean through his satire, sarcasm, irony, and humor. Along with the
above, he employs caricature in presenting the "complex fate of the
Caribbean," while Harris, John Hearne, Lamming, Andrew Salkey, and Selvon
pursue the rebuilding of the native's cultural image (Bhatnager 30-31), and
each uses different techniques. Walcott focuses on the socio-political,
economic, and cultural struggle which results from the Caribbean cultural
pluralism. Walcott's artistic and dramatic approach incorporates his mulatto
metaphor to depict the freshness and uniqueness of the Caribbean, while
Braithwaite uses a historical and poetic approach that has been immersed in
Afrocentricism to advance the theory of knowing one's history in order to find
one's identity and to achieve one's destiny. Lamming uses a Marxist approach
to focus on the working class which, he believes, will overthrow the
oppressors. Michael Anthony forces his readers to look at the Caribbean from
a different point of view, and then he asks about the future of the postcolonial
Caribbean.

The historical and cultural diversity influences the writers' thematic and
stylistic choices, and this becomes the strength of these writers. For example,
Naipaul's cynical and negative portrayal of the Caribbean's development finds
its opposite and complement in Walcott's creative and positive portrayal. Naipaul postulates in *A Bend in the River*: "The world is what it is; men who are

nothing, who allow themselves to become nothing, have no place in it" (3). This statement follows a similar note in his famous statement in *The Middle Passage* that "history is built around achievement and creation; and nothing was created in the West Indies" (29), as well as it links with the displacement of his characters. But Walcott rejects such a pessimistic view of the Caribbean by counteracting that "if there was nothing, there was everything to be made. With this prodigious ambition one began" ("What the Twilight Says" 4). Cynically, Naipaul may reply, building what? The thing Popo builds? "The thing without a name?" (*Miguel Street* 17–25). Yet such diverse perspectives do enhance the growth of Caribbean literature, as well as world literature. Robert Hamner perceives that "although the two [Naipaul and Walcott] take opposite positions on crucial issues, they are actually complementary and necessary to each other in rendering a complete picture of the West Indies" ("Aspects of National Character" 179).

## History

In the Caribbean, Lamming and Walcott advocate a combination of traditional and modern, yet each approach is vastly different. Lamming argues in *In the Castle of My Skin*, that a denial of history leads to the loss of identity. The villagers neither want to hear about nor discuss past slavery. For this reason they have no clearly defined path for the future of postcolonialism after ownership of land is passed from the British landlord to the new elite of the working class.

Walcott uses himself, a mulatto, as a central metaphor to depict the Caribbean's problem and solution. A merging of his African and European heritage, in *Another Life*, is needed to deal with the problems of slavery and colonialism. Lamming further uses a post-colonial interpretation of *The Tempest* to demonstrate a new perspective, one which "is demystified as an intellectual process that resituates the colonial writer as an active agent of decolonization" (Paquet X).

## Language

From this new and appropriated perspective, there is no argument about Caribbean writers' use of the colonizers' languages versus the use of their native languages. Rather, these writers confidently and forcefully use English in their own way as a tool and weapon to carve out their destiny.

Wilentz points out that "unlike the former colonies in Africa or India... there was no language native to the Caribbean after the almost complete genocide of the Amerindians" (261). In her essay, "English Is a Foreign Anguish," Wilentz illustrates "how Caribbean writers have disrupted the colonial language and adopted it as a language of opposition" (262), but she also alludes to the painful experience of these writers. For example, Harris postulates how he has disrupted and appropriated the colonizer's language:

> I am not at all engaged in a politics of protest against the language of the so-called imperialist master. History within my mixed antecedents, across conflicting generations, has brought the supreme blessing of a language I genuinely love. A living language is a medium for which one must be profoundly grateful. English in which I write my novels, is my native language not because of historical imposition or accident but because of numinous proportions that sustain originality within a living text. ("The Fabric of the Imagination" 19)

Having made such a bold comment, it is not contradictory for Harris to admit to the subtle complexities facing the Caribbean writers. In a seminar at the University of Texas in 1982, Harris explained his anguish: "I had to unlearn what I had learned. I could not just write 'The river is dark; the tree is green.' One of the tasks that began to hurt me personally is how to write that" (qtd. in Wilentz 268).

Because of the many variations of vocabulary, rhythm, register, intonation, dialect, ideolect, slang, and jargon, different complexities arise in the use of English. Jean D'Costa illustrates the dilemma facing the Caribbean writers:

> The (Caribbean) writer operates within a polydialectal continuum with a creole base. His medium, written language, belongs to the sphere of standardized language which exerts a pressure within his own language community while embracing the wide audience of international standard English... . If the writer is to satisfy himself, his local audience and that wider international audience, he must evolve a literary dialect which will meet the following: the demands for acceptability within and without his own community, and the pressure for authentic representation of the language culture of his own community. ("The West Indian Novelist and Language" 252)

Most of the first generation of Caribbean writers are still affected by the switching complexities of slavery and colonization, during which time several territories experienced several cultures and languages—namely Dutch, Spanish, French, and English. Then the confluence of Africa, Europe, and India in the Caribbean produced not only physical and cultural mulattoes, but also linguistic mulattoes. Walcott, a notable mulatto example, expresses this cultural and linguistic tension in "A Far Cry From Africa." He has both African and British heritages. Rather than allowing the two extremes to create further conflict, however, he seeks to use them as a positive complement. Walcott's linguistic tension is further demonstrated in his plays. Commenting on Walcott's linguistic dilemma in *Dream on Monkey Mountain*, Ismith Khan, a Caribbean writer, indicates that none of his characters could possibly speak with the "sophistication, the erudition and the poetry which are emulations of British standards," but since Walcott is "loathe to cut things out or throw things away, he twists, bends, and forces extraneous elements into the body of his work—he must have those lines, even though they are in a language, meter, and rhythm totally alien to his characters and their lives" (149). Khan's argument continues to point out that "had the writer gone to the extreme end of the spectrum of West Indian dialect," the play would not have been understood by American and British audiences. Yet the cry of the post-colonial Caribbean has been for literature that is "autonomous, nationalistic, and homegrown." But Walcott "has pigeonholed himself before he even begins" (149). This "pigeonholing" of Walcott is the experience of most Caribbean writers "because no one writes for the bottom drawer" (152). Khan and several other Caribbean writers have dialect novels in their "bottom drawers" because of negative reactions from editors and publishers (152).

They have developed a language mastery, in the face of shifting circumstances, which is the "nature of cultural behaviour in the Caribbean creole continua," where a language shift becomes a behavioral shift, resulting in a meaning shift (D'Costa, "Expression and Communication" 124). D'Costa further illustrates the intricacy of this language mastery by Caribbean writers:

> The (Caribbean) writer confronts in his own mind the array of possible language forms which arise at the bidding of any single notion he may wish to express. At this partially conscious level he must sift the mental events, emotions, and patterns of association within him such that the ideal balance of meaning may be achieved. This suggests a kind of language competence in which variation, code-switching and minimal shifting form a complete whole rather than clearly separated systems realizing themselves in different surface structures. ("The West Indian Novelist and Language" 256)

# Conclusion

As a result of the very nature of its historical, social, political, and cultural experiences, Caribbean Literature records a uniquely complex richness of literary content and form, and this complex richness deflates a narrow, parochial perspective and reflects a multiplicity of interdisciplinarity, intertextuality, and multiculturalism. In telling and retelling the missing, distorted, and silenced narratives of oppressed peoples, Caribbean writers offer intriguing perspectives on the particular and the universal conditions of humanity. In terms of interdisciplinarity they employ poetry and prose to create a mosaic of science, politics, history, psychology, language, culture, painting, and literature. Textually their works depict layers, shades, and depths of biblical, classical, and contemporary allusions, thereby further enriching their works of art. These works as well as their authors are products of slavery and colonization, but the authors have positively appropriated from the past with a kind of postcolonial write back and a "colonization in reverse" (Bennett). Yet, the authors and their texts reflect a unique indigenous creativity far surpassing the expectation of colonial and canonical agents.

Culturally Caribbean writers use their rich cultural mixture as literary explorations of global diversity with fresh imagination. Harris, for example, uses his African, European, and Amerindian heritage to advance these explorations, and focuses on the imagination to transcend conventions into new "discoveries and creations" (Boxill 190). His 1983 *The Womb of the Space* with its appropriate subtitle *The Cross-Cultural Imagination* captures not only Harris' intention, but other Caribbean writers' postcolonial and multicultural reevaluation and creation.

# CHAPTER TWO

# Synonymy of Multiculturalism and Postcolonialism through Globalization

In *End of Empire*, Brian Lapping concludes that "with the end of the British Empire came the end of all empires. To conquer lands and rule them from a home base was widely regarded as legitimate before the twentieth century. The British were the last of the great subjugators with the self-confidence to call their conquests an Empire" (xv). Under the British colonial system, there was a flow of population and ideas from the West outwards, and educational curricula in colonial societies reflected a parochial concentration and a homogeneous approach appropriate for a monolithic culture, but inappropriate for multiculturalism. This approach, therefore, left natives in more than two thirds of the world in a state of emptiness and powerlessness (Ashcroft, Griffiths, and Tiffin 1-3). It also suppressed the fluidity of identities in the colonies, and silenced a multitude of voices. The latter half of the twentieth century, however, has ushered in not only the independence of many former British colonies, but also postcolonial studies, multiculturalism, and globalization. In an age of globalization, when colonization is in reversed, postcolonial deconstruction examines and re-examines the effects of slavery, transplantation, suppression, and marginalization (Ashcroft, Griffiths, and Tiffin 1-3).[1]  But as a continuing process of resistance and reconstruction, postcolonialism, aided by globalization, demonstrates the irrelevance and obsolescence of educational and cultural homogeneity, arguing forcefully for multiculturalism and heterogeneity, especially in the studies of literature and criticism. Chapter two seeks to develop this argument, and it will demonstrate the rationale, methodology, and result of this position through reference to postcolonial theory, criticism, history, and transnational literatures.

## Colonialism

Colonialism, or to be more specific, British Imperialism has been defined by many historians, anthropologists, theorists, critics, and writers from different angles. Depending on which sides of the fence critics are on, they see or allow themselves to see their sides or perspectives of colonialism. It is still a shock, even though it should not shock us, to hear academic and critical debates and arguments in favor of slavery and colonization. George Nadel and Perry Curtis, for example, explains:

> Whereas "imperialism" enjoyed at least a genuine if fleeting respectability, "colonialism" has been weighed down with original sin almost since its inception. To some, colonialism has meant imperialism as seen from the colonial vantage point; and indeed, that all colonialisms have been implied by imperial expansion, but that not all imperial expansions imply colonialism, is undeniable. (3)

They further point out that while "colonialism" is commonly used to mean the "oppression, humiliation, or exploitation of indigenous peoples," it should also be used to show the positive side, for example, "transporting and modifying of European institutions overseas; colonial policies and administrative practices ... and the opposition within the mother country to owning colonies" (3). In harmony with this argument, Herbert Luthy argues in his article, "Colonization and the Making of Mankind," that colonialism is a vituperative word, so he prefers the word *colonization* to describe how civilization and culture were taken to underdeveloped countries to raise the standards of these countries to present levels (27).[2] However, Dr. Emanuel Moresco provides a more objective understanding of the origin of colonialism. To Moresco, "colonies resulted from the migration of men to areas outside their ordinary habitat" (21). He differentiates various types of migration which include migrations within the state,

> expansion to contiguous territories...migrations of entire peoples to form new homes; partial movement of a people...movement of groups of individuals into another country ... and migration to countries where the colonists remain subject to the supreme authority of the home country, which then becomes the metropolitan power in relation to that country. (21)

Whatever are the differences in meanings and perspectives, they do not and cannot refute the fact that British Imperialism ruled the colonies with force and homogeneity,[3] even though these colonies were some of the most heterogeneous nations and continents. My use of homogeneity in British rule means ruling in a kind of deliberate blindness that is profitable for the colonizer, but detrimental for the colonized. A very good example of this is the creation of federations in Asia, Africa, and the West Indies. From 1935, the grand scheme was to create the federation. Even as late as the 1960s attempts were made to create a federation in Africa. In the case of the West Indies, from the nineteenth century to the late twentieth century, attempts were made by the British to create the West Indian Federation. From 1945 onwards, the Colonial office gave serious thoughts towards the formation of the West Indian Federation, but all attempts were failed because of money and power (Louis, Discussion, August 1, 2000). Other homogenous methods of rule and control include the political, cultural, economic, and military systems. In 1939, for example, "the Viceroy of India declared war against Germany on behalf of all the 400 million people of India and its 650 princes. He did not consult a single Indian. That was imperial power" (Lapping xiv).[4] But the conflict was that countries in Africa, Asia, and the Caribbean were/are richly diverse in language and culture. Thus, the superimposed homogenous rule created national and individual cultural, economic, and political conflicts.

Economic profit was at the center of British Imperialism according to Ronald Edward Robinson and John Gallagher's *Africa and the Victorians: The Official Mind of Imperialism* (1961), Walter Rodney's *How Europe Underdeveloped Africa* (1974), and A. J. Hopkins and Peter Cain's *European Imperialism: Crisis and Deconstruction, 1914–1990* (1993) and *British Imperialism: Innovation and Expansion, 1688–1914* (1993). Gopal demonstrates how Britain and India fitted together in colonial domination since Britain was the world leader in trade and manufacture, and India supplied cotton and jute to British factories, indigo and opium for markets, and railways for British investors and manufacturers. Further, "India's export surplus was utilized to balance Britain's deficits with Europe and the United States; but British capital was mostly invested in 'white settler' countries" (13). As a result of such gross exploitation, the annual per capita income in 1875 was about 2, and approximately 29 millions Indians died of starvation between 1854 and 1901 (13). Walter Rodney adds that Britain's surplus from Africa in 1934 provided social services for the British at six pounds 15 shillings per person, but less than one shilling nine pence per Nigerian (206). Lapping concurs, "profit motive" led to the "creation of the Empire," and "led also to the final decision to let it go under, in the most places, without a fight" (538).

By duplicating the same or similar political, cultural, and educational system for all her colonies, Britain made less and cheap labor for the expatriates, but a traumatic nightmare for the colonized, who found it increasingly problematic to discover and define themselves.[5] The colonizer's perspective attained supremacy over the colonized's views, needs, and differences. They suppressed the colonized's heterogeneity into a homogeneous prison, and they built their own homogeneous communities in the colonies. This is the world into which neither the upper middle class Indian doctor, Aziz, in *A Passage to India* can enter, nor can the boys on San Christobal, in *In the Castle of My Skin* enter the soldiers' party.[6] It is this militarily and culturally created homogenous community of security for the British in India at the time of Gandhi's "quit India" campaign, that Daphne Manners is raped when she steps out of the homogeneity of the collective raj. Janis Tedesco and Janet Popham point out that "as feelings of insecurity increased, their collective instincts took command. The raj as a group began to matter more than the raj as individuals" (xi). This group of British Whites in Northern and Southern Rhodesia rally together as one group for strength and survival. In *The Raj Quartet* a similar pattern takes shape:

> But survival depended on racial purity. The raj could not contaminate themselves by becoming too closely involved with India and black natives. They cultivated, isolated, and jealously guarded their cantonments which mirrored, as closely as possible, the environment of their island homeland. And yet the raj were as isolated from the intellectual and cultural climate of England as they were from black India. They were exiles without a home, rulers without a purpose or justification. (Tedesco and Popham xii)

But they turned this position into one from where they would rule with force and strength because homogeneity strengthens the colonizer's "self-confidence and self-sufficiency," and as a result of this "self-confidence" and "self-sufficiency," they are protected from the dangers of losing their sense of identity through submergence, assimilation, and influence. Their "distinctiveness and uniqueness are preserved" (Mohabir 70-71). However, the "natives," as they are called, are lumped into one homogeneous group of the "other," thereby disregarding their color, flavor, distinctiveness, and heterogeneity. Colonial essentializing, therefore, laid the foundation for racially stereotyping the colonized as lazy, weak, "wicked, backward," "evil, thievish," "sadistic," irresponsible, extravagant, and "incompatible with one another" (Memmi 79-89).

Ruling people as one group relieves the pressures and problematizations of "unfamiliar questions and issues" and "tensions" and "misunderstandings about customs, values, moral norms and experiences" (Mohabir 70), but the complication of this homogeneous approach is that these people are not one group. In India, there are many languages and religions. There are great gulfs among castes. Africa is similar. Middle Easterners disagree violently over political and religious issues. Walcott describes the origin of Caribbean heterogeneous composition as an inheritance of a rich social and cultural milieu of slavery, indentureship, and colonization. The Nobel literature laureate describes the Caribbean as a vase made of pieces broken off from several cultures ("Nobel lecture" 31). The Caribbean, therefore, through its colorful and diverse celebrations like carnival and mashramani,[7] becomes a symbol of diversification and deracialization. Critic and writer, Wilson Harris, adds another constructive dimension to the colony's heterogeneity in his 1983 *The Womb of the Space* with its appropriate subtitle *The Cross-Cultural Imagination* capturing Harris' intention: "The paradox of cultural heterogeneity, or cross-cultural capacity, lies in the evolutionary thrust it restores to orders of the imagination, the ceaseless dialogue it inserts between hardened conventions and eclipsed or half-eclipsed otherness, within an intuitive self that moves endlessly into flexible patterns, areas or bridges of community" (xviii). But by treating the colony as one large homogeneous group, the colonizer weakens the psyche of the colonized, and leaves them in a state of dependency, "dependency complex," "colonizability" (Memmi 88–89). These oral, multiracial, and multicultural societies enrich each other through their rich community lifestyle, but when "complementarity is inevitably lost through [forced] exclusiveness," and "there is little [or no] opportunity for cross-fertilization of ideas" and resources, then the colonized's sense of identity is further destroyed, placing them in greater vulnerability for exploitation and domination (Mohabir 70–71). Rochester's inability and refusal to acknowledge Antoinette's rich cultural heterogeneity leads him into a racial, cultural, and sexual paranoid homophobia; which becomes his alibi to execute his patriarchal and Eurocentric forced exclusion of Antoinette from love and life—Christophine, Sandy, Blacks, the landscape, and the Caribbean.[8] Frantz Fanon describes this colonial phenomenon as alienation from the other (*Wretched of the Earth*).

British Imperialism developed a rubber-stamped system for colonial rule and colonial education. In "Education and Neocolonialism," Philip Altbach argues that neocolonialism has replaced the old colonial educational system, but in a more subtle manner. Under colonialism, "indigenous educational patterns" were replaced by foreign ones to foster the dependency syndrome. Inadequacies, lack of technological advances, deficiencies in personnel and curricular spheres were frequent in colonial education (453). The educational system was like a colonial funnel (filtering) system designed to train a few to be loyal to the British in ruling the masses. The first major filtering begins with your class, color, and religion. These will determine which preparatory and elementary schools one will attend. The second filtering is in standard four where on an average less than 10 percent will pass the Common Entrance Examination for admission to secondary or high schools. Of course the majority of schools receive less than 10 percent because they are not the elite schools. They are in the country and rural areas where the facilities are outrageously poor. The majority of students who fail CEE already realize that they have to look elsewhere for a livelihood. Some may get a second chance by passing the Preliminary Certificate Examination in Form Two or the College of Preceptors Examination in Form Four. Passing these, depending on the students' age, can still get the students into secondary schools, but by then the "real high school" students have already had two or four years, respectively, of new subjects like foreign languages and science and social science subjects. These PCE or CPE students can still get a fairly decent job like teaching in a rural school or mail carrier, but only few, through private study, improved their status. The third major filtering takes place at the end of fifth form when students write the London Exams, General Certificate Examination at "O" level. Few students get the right number and the appropriate subjects (generally five subjects including English and Math) to proceed to do General Certificate Examination at "A" level, or to go to university, or to get a job. At the GCE "A" level results, in the case of the Caribbean countries including Guyana, less than 15 students from the entire nation would be fairly successful, with only three to six gaining the country's scholarships. Such an inappropriate and imposed system has helped few, but harmed the masses by leaving them in illiteracy, ignorance, and poverty. But this situation aids the colonizer's strategy of keeping the masses in a state of dependency as pointed out in *Pedagogy of the Oppressed*. Under such system Elias, in *Miguel Street*, has to settle for a scavenger's job instead of a civil servant's position because of his repeated failures with the British Exams.[9]

Another strategy of oppression by colonial education is in the area of history. Denial of history—history of the colonies and the colonized—further undermined the voice and identity of the colonized. Additionally, the imposition of the colonizer's history, in a Eurocentric methodology, on students from the colonies facilitated imperial control and manipulation, which led to the colonized's distrust of history (Kennedy 350). Furthermore, colonization removed the colonized from history (Rodney), and to be removed from history and the community, according to Memmi, was the "most serious blow suffered by the colonized" (91). For this reason, Walcott insists that his "memory cannot summon any filial love" ("Muse" 373–74).

Denial, deception, and disruption of history increased the colonized's vulnerability to be racially branded, labeled, and stereotyped. Colonialist literature became a key tool to achieve the colonizer's objective of essentializing the colonized and reducing them to a state of inferiority.[10] German, French, Spanish, and English literature had unlimited scope to describe and define the colonized. German writers, for example, stereotyped the colonized: "The 'Natives' smell, are lazy, are impulsive and childish, they are utterly indifferent to morality, they are said to welcome a beating if they have deserved it'—in short, all the shallow, protective clichés of the colonial mind went towards German fiction's account of relations with the Africans" (Ridley 73). For instance, Frieda Kraze's novel, *Heim Neuland* (1909), tells about a German couple visits an African celebration, but then underscores the Africans:

> These people were not human beings. Not even those of them who had become Christians.... That was proved by the fact that their character had not changed, by their sadistic brutality and their frequent lapses into hereditary primitiveness. Perhaps in a few hundred years time they might become human beings, but for the present they were no better than animals. (2)

Hugh Ridley argues that the author "clearly shares this view, for her novel ignores Africans from that moment on" because that is the moment when all colonial writers "decided that the colonized people were utterly alien and could be spoken of as they had no human characteristics at all" (73-74). He further illustrates that British colonial writers depicted India and Africa as sexual and savage. "These attitudes," Ridley continues, "had a long history. From the sixteenth century the encounter with dark-skinned peoples had created in the European mind pictures of semi-humans driven by sensual, bestial passion" (74).

Octave Mannoni, Frantz Fanon, Richard Wright and other postcolonial critics and writers have examined this racial stereotype in the areas of sex. White European women on the colonies were protected and insulated through Eurocentric homogeneity, in order to protect white males' fear of losing on the sexual battleground to the men of color. In a humorous and ironic tone, Florence King describes how Southern men toast to Southern women's sexual coldness, but uses it as an excuse for racial delinquency. As an example, she cites a passage from a newspaper: "To Woman, lovely woman of the Southland, as pure and chaste as this sparkling water, as cold as this gleaming ice, we lift this cup, and we pledge our hearts and our lives to the protection of her virtue and chastity." She then translates the real meaning of the passage: "To Woman, without whose purity and chastity we could never have justified slavery and segregation, without whose coldness we wouldn't have had the excuse we needed for messing around down in the slave cabins and getting plenty of poontang. We pledge our hearts and our lives to the protection of her virtue and chastity because they are the best political leverage we ever did see" (38). Although King's *Southern Ladies and Gentlemen* derives humor through irony in depicting the changing South in the middle of the twentieth century, the point about race and sex is critical in colonialism. Colonialist writers have condemned interracial marriage and sex. The men and women of color were depicted as the "depraved," with "insatiable sexual appetite," who would corrupt the colonizer (Ridley 75-76). The writers were concerned about two issues: "the danger of the white man and his ethos" and "the danger of the colony" (76).[11] This mythical phenomenon convinces Roony and the British community that Adela Quested has been raped by Aziz in the Marabar Caves. Forster himself leaves the question delicately open-ended which is a great literary technique to manipulate human curiosity, especially in the area of sex. But for the colonized the law is guilty until proven innocent. Salman Rushdie adds that "where Forster's scene in the Marabar Caves retains its ambiguity and mystery, Scott gives us not a rape but a gang assault, and are perpetuated, what is more, by peasants" (89). Similarly, Bigger Thomas is tried and executed, not so much on the basis of his two murders, but on the suspicion that he has raped Mary Dalton and burned her body to destroy evidences.[12] Naked black bodies of Big Boy and his friends before a terrified, screaming southern white woman is a convincing attempted rape warranting shooting from a soldier's fiance.[13] The fear that Sandi, Antoinette's cousin from the colony, has had sex with Antoinette sends Rochester into hysteria, leading to a series of punitive and irrational actions—sex with Amelie beside Antoinette's room, alienation of Antoinette from her community, control of her money, and removal of Antoinette from the island.

According to S. Ekema Agbaw, "the late 19th and early 20th century was the climax of European colonialism in Africa, when white traders, missionaries, travelers, colonial administrators, anthropologists and creative writers presented Africans as negations of themselves" (134). These portraits were, mostly, limited and inaccurate because of the failure of the English to understand most people from different races and cultures (Street 3), and their portraits were dependent on secondary sources from science and literature. For example, John Buchan's *Prester John* (1910), reinforces "Africa as the dark continent, mysterious, romantic, dangerous, peopled by inferior savages, primitive and centuries behind Europeans in social and moral evolution, but consumed by instincts and passions which the civilized Europeans are more able to control" (qtd. in Joffe 77).[14] Even Charlotte Bronte becomes a servant to the "axiomatics of imperialism," in the creation of the "human/animal Bertha Mason (Spivak 121). Jane Eyre clearly reiterates the dominant colonial perspective of the natives from the colony: "In the deep shade, at the further end of the room, a figure ran backwards and forwards. What it was, whether beast or human being, one could not ... tell: it groveled, seemingly, on all fours; it snatched and growled like some strange wild animal: but it was covered with clothing, and a quantity of dark, grizzled hair, wild as a mane, hid its head and face" (295). Bronte and Jane's perception of the "other" as animal is typical of the colonizer and colonialism. To add to Jane's imagery of the colony as depraved, Bronte gives Rochester a subsequent passage where he sees the Caribbean as hell and Europe as heaven, similar to Marlow's concept of Africa and Europe:

"One night I had been awakened by her yells ... it was a fiery West Indian night .... 'This life,' said I at last, 'is hell! – this is the air–those are the sounds of the bottomless pit! I have a right to deliver myself from it if I can.... Let me break away, and go home to God!'"

"A wind fresh from Europe blew over the ocean and rushed through the open casement: the storm broke, streamed, thundered, blazed, and the air grew pure.... It was true Wisdom that consoled me in that hour, and showed me the right path ....

"'Go,' said Hope, 'and live again in Europe.... You have done all that God and Humanity require of you.'" (310-11)

Thus, by the mid-nineteenth century a racially stereotyped portrait of the colonized was already established (Street 6).[15] Many critics, including Agbaw and Phil Joffe, feel that this practice has continued throughout the 20th century. For example, as recent as 1985 in the historic documentary, *End of Empire*, several British officials and officers who served in different colonies would still describe the colonized in stereotypical manner. Sir Peter Rohobotham, commenting on Iran's nationalization of the oil industry, claimed that no amount of teaching could make the Iranians learn how to operate the industry because they "could never understand it" (Section on Iran). Philip Mohabir describes an incident where a Scandinavian Christian visited Guyana and after the first day with the Guyanese loggers, he described them as indiscipline and lazy, but after his actual involvement in the logging, "half way through the second day he returned earlier than the rest, looking very distressed indeed." Later, he confessed how wrong he was to pre and misjudge the men (151-52).

## Multiculturalism

Roger Matuz defines multiculturalism as "a social ideology predicated on the belief that no system of values is innately superior to any other" (361). Emerging from the civil rights movement in the 1960s and collaborating with feminism in the 1970s, multiculturalism developed "a strong reaction against the idealization of Eurocentric and male-dominated orthodoxies to a movement with profound academic, social, and political complications" (Matuz 361). Advocates of multiculturalism like Toni Morrison, Derek Walcott, Wilson Harris, Henry Louis Gates, Jr., Nina Baym, Barbara H. Smith, and John Guillory argue that American culture is incoherent without acknowledgment of the contributions from other racial, ethnic, and cultural groups. They further claim that multiculturalism is "a legitimate means" to address such "vital issues as racism, sexism, economic polarization and social fragmentation" (qtd. in Matuz 361). Allan Bloom's *The Closing of the American Mind: How Higher Education Has Failed Democracy and Impoverished Souls of Today's Students*, published in 1988, gave impetus and spark to the momentum of multiculturalism. Bloom argues that the greatness and the great achievements of the United States of America are due to America's dependence on and preservation of traditional Western books, art, values, and principles. Such archaic and dogmatic argument is out of step with cultural and technological innovations, but it does serve as a kind of colonial linkage. Further, traditional literary canonization is the strength of the new neo-colonialist empire, but canon expansion and multiculturalism will decolonize any narrow-minded, repressive system. Critics and writers like Maria Margaronis, Toni Morrison, Derek Walcott, Chinua Achebe, Wilson Harris, Mole Asanti, and others advance the cause for diversity and equality; while Dinesh D'Souza, William Bennett, and E. D. Hirsch are involved in a fight against multiculturalism in order to rebuild the walls of imperialism.

Winning the argument for or against multiculturalism, however, is pointless; what is important is the reality that according to the Census Bureau, in 1960, 90% of Americans were white, but by the year 2000 non-Hispanic whites are fewer than 60% of the population. Barna's research adds that Caucasian's population growth is at zero percent, while African American, Hispanic American, and Asian American are experiencing double-digit population growth. With this demographic shift, Caucasian population in the United States of America will fall below 50% by the year 2050 (2). Guyelberger's prophetic warning that any curriculum that ignores the importance of literature from the other world—the Third World, or postcolonial world, would be obsolete and parochial ("Decolonizing the Canon" 508). Margaronis advises that "in the din of reaction, it's easy to forget our real advantage: America is multicultural; sooner or later, the old guard will have to come to terms with what that means, and it won't just be about which books to read at school" (17). There is a wind of change that is blowing all across the world. This wind has orchestrated the synonymy of multiculturalism and postcolonialism in an era of globalization. The stage is set. Another Act of the play must begin.

## Globalization

Urbanization has brought more than half of the world's population huddled together in the large cities. Globalization, especially through technologically advanced transportation and communication, has reduced the world to a global village. Speaking about the importance and implication of cross-cultural witness in a global world, Mohabir claims that "the globalisation and urbanisation of our society has changed its complexion and composition. In this cosmopolitan scene," he advises, "we need to widen our horizons so that we can take advantage of the present situation and remain relevant" (70). In colonial times the West came to the colonies through old and rough sea and land routes over a long period of time. Mailbox and telegram were the main communication instruments. To the colonies, Britain was a mystery since it was inconceivable. Christophine describes England as the cardboard world that does not exist because she cannot see it. This colonial mystique held many colonies–India, African nations, and West Indian islands–in a state of colonial hypnosis and paralysis as depicted in Kipling's *The Man Who Would be King*. But through education and resistance, nationalists–though frequently demonized by British imperial propaganda–broke the myth. The once colonized now see themselves as equal to the colonizer. Today, the colonies are pouring into the West faster and in larger quantities due to the advancement of technology. Further, ideas flow in both directions through the uses of fax, telephone, email, and internet, in a fast-paced digital and cyberspace world. Politicians and business people can be in two or more countries in the same day, and scholars can network on a science or art project with colleagues from around the world. Globalization as an isolated and insulated phenomenon, however, has potentials for construction and destruction, but as a network with postcolonial studies and multiculturalism, it situates itself in a strategic position to revolutionize the world in a healthy way by shining the light on dark areas of race, class, gender, religion, and education.

## Postcolonialism

Postcolonial studies–by postcolonial studies I mean postcolonial theory, literature, and criticism–constitutes "a major intervention in the widespread revisionist project that has impacted academia since the 1960s—together with such other counter discourses that are gaining academic and disciplinary recognition as cultural studies, women studies, Chicano studies, African American studies, gender studies, and ethnic studies" (Gugelberger, "Postcolonial Cultural Studies" 581). Postcolonial literature was always in existence once there was "interaction between imperial culture and the complex of indigenous cultural practices" (Ashcroft, Griffiths, and Tiffin 1), but was never given a recognizable expression because of the canonical control of the imperial press. Once colonized peoples had the opportunity to "reflect on and express the tension which ensued from this problematic and contested, but eventually vibrant and powerful mixture of imperial language and local experience," postcolonial studies gained recognition (1). Postcolonial studies, therefore, intends to "scrutinize" colonizer-colonized relationship, "resist," "reshape," "overhaul," colonial perspectives (Boehmer 3), and "decolonize the mind" of both the colonizer and the colonized (wa Thiong'o ); bringing to center of discussion "the interconnection of issues of race, nation, empire, migration and ethnicity with cultural production" (Moore-Gilbert 6). Furthermore postcolonial studies are long and tedious tasks of dialoguing with skill and wisdom into "European-made history" with the intention of correcting centuries of colonial distortion (Gugelberger, "Postcolonial Cultural Studies" 582). Most, if not all, postcolonial writers, theorists, and critics will arrive at this theoretical juncture, and will have to decide when and how to confront the Eurocentric mythology of colonialism. In the case of Africa, writers discovered that Eurocentric representation of their history and literature has been a gross misrepresentation of Africa as a primitive and unrecognized culture. These writers embraced the process of decolonization and re-creation. The scientist, writer, and diplomat Davidson Abioseh Nicol, from Sierra Leone, explained why he wrote: "Because I found that most of those who wrote about us seldom gave any nobility to their African characters unless they were savages or servants or facing impending destruction. I knew differently" (qtd. in Achebe, "Colonialist Criticism" 16). In fact, some writers, in reading European literature, once found themselves on the side of the colonizer. In an interview with Bill Moyers, Achebe revealed his enlightenment at the university of Ibadan. He suddenly realized that colonial texts had to be read in a "different light" because even a "very highly praised book" like *Heart of Darkness* dehumanizes Africans. Achebe realized that he was reading about himself as "one of those savages jumping up and down on the beach." Such painful realization compelled him to write "a different story" (qtd. in Gikandi 32). G. D. Killam records another incident of enlightenment in Achebe's life, similar to the above. Achebe's intention was to study medicine, but he switched to literature, when he was "prompted by a reading of Joyce Cary's depiction of Nigeria and Nigerian character in *Mister Johnson* (1939). Achebe's purpose in writing was to "set the record of Nigeria's (and by extension Africa's) encounter with colonial history straight, to write about his own people and for his own people" (*Africa in English Fiction* 1874-1939 pg.100).

Under this new global, multicultural, and postcolonial umbrella; color, flavor, difference, and uniqueness release and re-surface the heterogeneity of more than two thirds of the world; thereby restoring their history, voice, identity, and power. This heterogeneity, for Mohabir, "promotes wider understanding among peoples of different origins, understanding in which the seed bed of co-operation and tolerance can grow" (74-75). Understanding and tolerance, of course, were destroyed among the colonized by the colonizer.[16] Britain's role in and responsibility for ethnic, racial, and religious divides and disputes in Asia—particularly India, Pakistan, and Bangladesh in partition riots and independence struggles in the 1940s, Africa–Mau Mau riots in Kenya, CCP and NLM in the Gold Coast, and Nkomo and Mugabe in Southern Rhodesia, Middle East—Iran's struggle to own and control its means of production in the 1950s, and West Indies—Guyana's race riots in the early 1960s and struggle to gain independence. Such "divide and rule," or "divide and quit," policies by supposedly one of the religious world empire is in direct contradiction to biblical admonition. Paul declares to the Colossians: "there is no distinction between Greek and Jew, circumcised and uncircumcised, barbarian, Scythian, slave and freeman, but Christ is all, and in all" (3:11-12). According to Mohabir, "heterogeneous living provides us with an opportunity to see ourselves as we really are and to get to know others as they really are. Some will be surprised that unity begins with a consciousness of our differences" (75). This is what colonialism destroyed; but postcolonialism, multiculturalism, and globalization seek to restore.

What God did at the tower of Babel (Gen. 11) is what the colonial power revised and applied in the colonies. At Babel, God scattered a people of one language because of their evil motive—to glorify self instead of God, but at Pentecost (Acts 2) God reversed Babel by gathering and uniting peoples from different cultures, languages, and races. Colonialism attempted to homogenized the colonized heterogeneity; but for the purpose of divide and conquer by causing schizophrenia, mimicry, and madness. This is depicted in many areas such as politics, language, religion, and race. Careful postcolonial analyses of Britain's manipulation of the following political situations will reveal how the British misunderstood, confused, divided, and undermined their colonies: India's quest for independence leading to partition in the late 1940s, Guyana's press for independence leading to race riots in the early 1960s, Iran's struggle for nationalism and nationalization, Egypt's fight to rid itself of Britain, and Aden's battle for freedom from the British and Ghana's pursuit of independence. V. S. Naipaul's *The Mimic Men* illustrates a fictional account of imperialist divide and rule on the basis of race in Guyana. Ralph Singh and Brown are the fictional names for Cheddi Jagan and Forbes Burnham. The novel also explores the theme of mimicry in the colony. Likewise, Jean Rhys' *Wide Sagasso Sea* examines colonial madness. Rochester imposes madness on Antoinette with a strong patriarchal and Eurocentric hand, having completed the colonial rape—robbing her of identity, power, money, name, culture, relations, and place. Rochester's attitude and action are typical of British imperialism—get in, grab as much as you can, and get out when trouble starts. Wilson Harris' *A Palace of the Peacock* also describes the colonizer's rape of the land of its natural resources.

## Conclusion

Postcolonial studies, may I say, should not be a race for revenge, or a blame game. Rather, it should be a call for analytical reasoning: "Come let us reason together," says the prophet Isaiah (Isa. 53:6). Part of the postcolonial reassessment and reasoning involves going to different peoples, learning from them, serving them, planning with them, starting with what they know, building on what they have, learning by doing, teaching by showing, and valuing people more than things (Mohabir 81). If the colonized made the mistake of neglecting these, postcolonial peoples should not repeat them or make similar mistakes. For example, African Americans, as once enslaved and colonized, can be so preoccupied with their struggle, independence, voice, and power, that they can forget to be good neighbors to immigrants and Hispanic, Native, and Asian Americans. Descendants of slaves and indentured servants in the Caribbean should resist the temptation of becoming new masters of the Amerindians in Guyana and immigrant minorities, especially the Haitians in the Bahamas. Hindu majority can learn to respect and value Jewish, Muslim, and Christian minorities in India. Swedes and Australians have much more to do for their indigenous peoples' freedom and empowerment. Universities, particularly through their International Studies, can surf the waves of postcolonial, multicultural, and global studies rather than resist the wind of change. Wise and insightful university leadership would seek to jump into the saddle of the racing horse rather than hanging onto the tail of the dead/dying donkey. Churches, particularly through their foreign missions and evangelistic programs, should "go ye into all the world and preach the gospel" (Matt. 26:28), but should be more culturally informed and understanding than our predessors. "Ours is a golden opportunity," Mohabir concludes in *Worlds Within Reach: Cross-cultural Witness*, "as a Church of Christ, to arise and change the trend of our society and reach our peoples of all nations" (218).

# Notes

1. Not all Europeans are colonizers. There were and are Europeans who worked for and with the colonized for the good of the people.

2. I use the words colonialism and colonization to depict the colonizer's oppression and exploitation of the colonized. At no time do I concur with Herbert Luthy's use of the words.

3. My use of the word here suggests a mono-methodology. It is different from, though not contradictory to, Ania Loomba's point about "colonialism's heterogeneous practices." In pointing out the problematization of generalizing colonialism, especially since there are different kinds of colonial contacts, Loomba argues that:

   > there is always a certain amount of reduction in any attempt to simplify, schematize or summarize complex debates and histories, and the study of colonialism is especially vulnerable to such problems on account of colonialism's heterogeneous practices and impact over the last four centuries. Each scholar of colonialism, depending on her disciplinary affiliation, geographic and institutional location and identity, is likely to come up with a different set of examples, emphasis and perspective or the question. (xiii)

4. Sarvepalli Gopal notes 662 Indian princes in his book, *Jawaharlal Nehru: A Biography* (1976).

5. Today, this point is still debated by historians and critics. Those who admire colonialism are amazed at Britain's ability to rule a vast empire with so few people. The people from the colonies, however, are aware of Britain's Prospero-like dominance through imprisonments, advanced weapons, and diplomatic lies

6. References are to E. M. Forester's *A Passage to India* and George Lamming's *In The Castle of My Skin*, respectively.

7. These are national cultural festivals in Trinidad (February) and Guyana (May), respectively.

8. Reference is from Jean Rhys' *Wide Sargasso Sea*.

9. For a more analytical discussion of colonial education, see Deena's "Colonization and Canonization: Class Marginalization: Class Marginalization through Education 532–38."

10. "Colonialist literature in contrast was that which was specifically concerned with colonial expansion. On the whole it was literature written by and for colonizing Europeans about non-European lands dominated by them. It embodied the imperialists' point of view. . . . [It] was informed by theories concerning the superiority of European culture and the rightness of empire" (Boehmer 3).

11. Professor Ballhatchet's study *Race, Sex, and Class under the Raj* is instructive on this issue in relation to India.

12. See Seodial Deena's "The Irrationality of Bigger Thomas' World" for discussion of this point.

13. References to Bigger Thomas and Big Boy are from Richard Wright's *Native Son* and "Big Boy Leaves Home," in *Uncle Tom's Children*, respectively.

14. See Brian Street and Hugh Ridley for more elaboration of this point.

15. Colonial writers who were influenced by anthropology, love for exotic portraits, etc., include D. H. Lawrence, H. Rider Haggard, R. M. Ballantyne, John Buchan, and A. E. W. Mason. It should also be noted that Darwin's theory of evolution, *Origins of the Species* (1858) became a major influence on much of colonial literature from this period (Street 6–10).

16. The following passage from David Hume's *The Philosophical Works* (1748) illustrates white ethnocentricism's influence on Western philosophy:

> I am apt to suspect the negroes, and in general all the other species of men . . . to be naturally inferior to the whites. There never was a civilized nation of any other complexion than white, nor even any individual eminent either in action or speculation. No ingenious manufactures amongst them, no arts, no sciences. On the other hand, the most rude and barbarous of the whites, such as the ancient Germans, the present Tartars, have still something eminent about them, in their valour, form of government, or some other particular. Such a uniform and constant difference could not happen in so many countries and ages. . . . In Jamaica indeed they talk of one negroe as a man of parts and learning; but 'tis likely he is admired for very slender accomplishments, like a parrot, who speaks a few words plainly. (252)

17. Postcoloniality is defined as "that condition in which colonized peoples seek to take their place forcibly, or otherwise, as historical subjects" (Boehmer 3).

18. By tolerance, I do not mean a reversal where extremists now impose their special-interest agenda on others.

# CHAPTER THREE

# Centrality of Caribbean Literature Depicting Postcolonial and Multicultural Preoccupations

The Caribbean writers are concerned with the confrontation of history, belonging to a place, identity, escape and escapism, and change. The writers explore these and other concerns from a postcolonial and multicultural perspective. One of the central questions is, how do we confront our past, our past of slavery and indentureship, war, and loss? Wilson Harris, in *The Whole Armour* and *A Palace of the Peacock*, depicts that history is a system of words, not facts, and that the Caribbean, is not the first place of slavery for the Africans, but that they were already slaves in Africa. Braithwaite, in a book of poetry, *The Arrivants*, also explores the question, how do we confront our past? He divides the book in three sections; "Rights of Passage," which deals with the journey of Africans from Africa to the Caribbean as slaves; "Masks," which takes us back to Africa, exploring the culture of conditions of the Africans; and "Islands," which depicts slavery in the Caribbean.

Jean Rhys enters into the individual consciousness and shows the price that is paid for freedom. Antoinette is the victim of the same slave system, she has benefited from, because she desires black. Rochester is also a victim of the vicious, exploitative system, which leaves him a dismayed individual, who can only live by analyzing things.

Michael Anthony, in *The Year of San Fernando*, is also preoccupied with the confrontation of history. Gordon Rohlehr sees Francis as a type of the slave. Rohlehr claims that at first, the boy is just there then the Chandles become more dependent on him. One can clearly see this line of interpretation. Additionally, the novel further contributes to the question of history through Anthony's exploration of the passage of time, in a different way. In referring to seasons throughout the novel, he shows the stages of the canes, allows us to hear the rain falling on the zinc, and makes us feel the heat of the sun. Anthony makes the passage of time present to the human mind. Through the boy's consciousness of his own growth (he learns about people, and life, infatuates with Julia, and becomes independent), we view him coming into life, as Mrs. Chandles grows feeble and goes out of this life. I agree with Rohlehr, in depicting the political change of the Caribbean, he sees the parallel of Francis' growth from childhood to adolescence, to that of the Caribbean from colonialism to independence.

George Lamming advocates that a denial of history leads to isolation and loss of identity. The villagers in In the Castle of My Skin do not want to know about slavery. The system makes them deny their history, causing them to feel they are unique, but incapable of altering their situation. The system achieves this by damaging their perceptions. Their perception of themselves is strongly influenced by the way the landlord perceives them. This is a parallel to slavery. The slaves perceive themselves as objects of the masters, and once they remain objects, they cannot act. In order for them to act freely, they must become free agents. A good example of this, is when the men are about to strike the landlord, they cannot strike. They are objects of Mr. Slime, so they wait for his word, but the word of command does not come, because Mr. Slime himself is not free. Thus action is paralyzed, and a state of colonial impotence becomes reality. On the other hand, history is made one of the central issues at the beginning of the book, as the author criticizes the colonial education system.

Much of Caribbean literature is concerned with the importance of belonging to a place, and when this feeling of belonging is destroyed, a person's identity is lost. One can understand the writers' dilemma, since most of them are from the forties and fifties, when a great wave of migration occurred. They have experienced alienation and displacement, and their expression filtered into their writings, consciously or unconsciously. In Jean Rhy's Wide Sargasso Sea, for example, Antoinette desperately tries to escape from the negation of her life, and assert herself. She tries to answer the questions, "Who's there? Who are you?" The answering of the questions leads to the demonstration of this loss of identity, which operates in three ways.[1]

First, the loss of identity is demonstrated by the loss of a sense of place, or the failure to identify with the Caribbean landscape. Antoinette loves the landscape. She is strong and passionate in the Caribbean landscape, which consists of the hot sun, the green vegetation, running streams. She is in harmony with the landscape, while Rochester is threatened by the landscape. He sees it as a very hostile element, which he cannot control, and because he cannot control it, he becomes more insecure from being in the Caribbean landscape. His way of escape then is to separate Antoinette from the landscape. He takes her to England, where her sense of place is destroyed. However, she clings to her red dress. When she is in the red dress, she is trying to recreate the Caribbean landscape, which she has chosen to identify with as her place of belonging. Antoinette is not 'Beke' like Rochester, she is white, but different, because she loves the landscape, whereas Rochester can only love a thing if he possesses it, and he cannot possess the landscape. Additionally, Derek Walcott, in *Another Life*, talks about the task of sitting down and naming the Caribbean landscape, while Michael Anthony, in *The Year of San Fernando*, forces us to see the Caribbean landscape in a new way, a way that causes us to identify with it and appreciate it. He brilliantly describes the canefields, seasons, and rural and urban areas.

The second way in which this identity is lost is by the loss of name. Rochester forces a cold, passive identity on Antoinette by calling her Bertha, in order to displace the hot, passionate identity of the name 'Antoinette.' She rejects it, by insisting that her name is Antoinette, and later condemns it as obeah. In V.S. Naipaul's works, the concept of writing and change of name is an attempt to change identity. Naipaul uses this concept frequently in novels, such as *A House for Mr. Biswas*, *Mmic Men*, and *Mystic Masseur*. In *Moon on a Rainbow Shawl*, Charlie wants to name his baby, Churchill Spencer, while Esther wants to call him—Byron. In each case the name is associated with a political or artistic identity, which can bring them out of poverty.

The third way of loss of identity is by a divided self. Antoinette, a French Creole and West Indian, is warm, sympathetic, and passionate. Her white skin, her outer world, isolates her "white cockroach" and when she runs to Tia, her black friend, Tia throws a stone at her. Her passionate feelings, her rich inner world, are in tuned with the environment and the blacks, but alienates her from the whites, who calls her "white nigger." In the Caribbean, Antoinette's inner and out world are in harmony, but her outer world disagrees with her physical appearance. But in England her inner and outer world are at war, and her outer world agrees with her physical appearance. She rejects reality, the outer world in England, so her inner dreams flow out to her outer reality. Dreams become reality and reality becomes dreams, so she becomes mad in the eyes of society. Her insanity, though, is perfectly illusive and understandable. The discovery of self is that Antoinette initiates action. She sets the house on fire. This action comes just after her dreams on pages 185–188. In her final dream and action she consciously affirms her identity to leap from the burning house, not to "Bertha! Bertha!" but to Tia, her black friend, and black half.

Throughout her life she tries to allow the 'black part' of her life to be enjoyed, but is constantly suppressed, by her family, then Rochester. She and Tia boil green bananas, bathe in the stream, and she wears Tia's dress. Tia represents that part of her life she does not want to part with. When she is faced with marital problems; she resorts to black superstitions and obeah. She pleads with Christophine to fix her a 'love potion, to get Rochester to love her, even if it is one more time.

In fact, the black house servant, Christophine becomes her mother. Christophine's philosophy is what she sees exists, not what she cannot see. This is her attitude to England, which, she claims, does not exist. Antoinette believes this and experiences it. She cannot believe England is real.

Derek Walcott in his book of poems, *Another Life*, describes himself as a split personality. He is a mulatto, and is divided between the English and the black. He uses his dilemma as a central metaphor for the Caribbean's problems. The Caribbean is at war with the rich African culture, struggling to find form under the European system.

Loss of identity leads to displacement, another recurring theme in Caribbean literature. Since most of the writers, themselves, live in foreign countries and experience alienation, loneliness, and loss of culture, their writings reflect this displacement. Rochester is very much displaced in the Caribbean as Antoinette is in England. The West Indians in England, as described by Samuel Selvon, in *Lonely Londoners*, are good examples of this displacement. They lose themselves, their culture, and the sense of community. Although Moses tries to foster this community spirit, by allowing them to meet, eat, and sleep at his apartment, the community still disintegrates. This is one of the consequences they suffer for living in a foreign large city. Thus they become fragmented, and out of the fragmentation they live 'crippled lives.'

Another feature of Caribbean literature is the strong mother figure. The mother bears the responsibility of the family because the father is either absent from the home or he is dead. In the black working class, the experience of a single parent, mostly the mother, raising the family is almost heroic. Many of the Caribbean novels are set in the working class tradition, and so the mother emerges as a figure of strength.

Antoinette's mother becomes insane. In fact, she is so depressed by the death of her first husband, the periods of separation from her second husband, and the chaotic slavery situations that she offers Antoinette very little help. It is Christophine, the black house servant, who becomes her mother, and a figure of strength. When Antoinette is faced with marital problems, she turns to Christophine for strength, counsel, and help. With Christophine by her side she is strong, but Rochester is threatened and insecure, so he sends Christophine away. Without Christophine, Antoinette crumbles. She cannot cope with her problems. Jean Rhys' characterization of Christophine is convincing. She is credible in her strength, and although little physical description is given of her, one hears the rhythm of her speech as powerful as one feels her presence: "Get up, girl, and dress yourself. Woman must have spunks to live in this wicked world" (101).

Escape and escapism is another area of focus in Caribbean literature. History, politics, and the socio-economic system of the Caribbean actually force West Indians in a so-called safe mode of escape psychologically, spiritually, and physically. In *Lonely Londoners* the people are desperate to get out of the Caribbean and to get to England. It matters little how they arrive in England and what conditions they have to endure, once they escape from the Caribbean. For example Henry arrives in England without resources, while Cap and Galahad have to capture seagulls and pigeons to eat, in order to survive. Bruce King, literary critic of Caribbean literature, says of these characters, "They escape into illusion. Various political and religious movements spring up and offer a sense of drama and excitement" (*West Indian Literature*, 100). Similarly, in *In The Castle of My Skin*, the head teacher escapes from his family failures and problems by drinking and beating the students. Mr. Slime escapes into politics, and at the end G leaves for a job in Trinidad.

*Miguel Street* and *Moon on a Rainbow Shawl* explore the theme of escape and escapism in a greater dimension. Rosa, Sophia, Mavis, Charlie, and Ephraim, the major characters of *Moon on a Rainbow Shawl* seek various forms of escape. Mavis escapes into a life of prostitution, while Sophia takes refuge in religious songs and abusive language to Charlie and Mavis. Rosa, pregnant with Ephraim's child, escapes into the materialistic world of Old Mack, for security reasons, while Charlie, disillusioned by the cricketing authority's silencing him for his voice for justice, escapes into drunkenness. Ephraim, who is more conscious and worried about his trapped situation, desperately fights to escape from the viciousness of the system. He flees to Liverpool, England.

In *Miguel Street*, Bogart, without roots, attempts to escape the futility of his "little room," in which he wastes his life playing patience. To escape from his boredom, he tries to get into the larger world, which is associated with Americans and Hollywood. On another level, Popo, one of the artist figures, fails to achieve his unattainable goals, and with the failures of his family life, he escapes into trying to create the thing without a name. "And yet Popo was never idle. He was always busy hammering and sawing and planing.... 'What you making, Mr. Popo?' I asked. Popo would always say, 'Ha, boy! That's the question. I making the thing without a name'" (17). Yet on another level, George fails to manage his family, he bullies them, and beats his wife to her death. When these fail to satisfy his frustrations, he sets up a brothel for American soldiers. He dies penniless. His son, Elias, in frustration and failure of the examinations, escapes into the job of a scavenger. He says, "No theory here...this is practical. I really like the work" (45).

B. Wordsworth, Laura, Man Man, Edward, Mr. Bhakhu, Big Foot, Mr. Morgan, Eddoes, Bolo, and even Hat become disillusioned and seek various from of escapism. Eventually, the narrator himself escapes by leaving the Caribbean. Laban Erapu says of the theme of *Miguel Street*: "What links the stories, and therefore the characters together, is the similar destiny of seemingly inevitable disillusionment in which they all wind up. This builds up the pattern of the whole novel, which ends on a similar note as the disillusioned narrator makes his own escape to a large world than the limited and limiting Miguel Street. Thus escape by the end becomes the main theme" (xii).

Change is another concern of Caribbean literature. This change may either be physical change, political change, social change, or spiritual change. In most cases there is a change in one's thinking, since Caribbean literature aims at revolutionizing one's consciousness. Antoinette, in her room, in England, is imprisoned, but she goes through a revolution in her consciousness, and as a result of the change, she initiates action. She sets the house on fire.

In *The Year of San Fernando*, physical, social, and political changes are interwoven. Francis' physical and social changes from childhood to adolescence parallel the emergence of the Caribbean from colonialism to independence. Francis' return to Mayaro, after one year in San Fernando, raises questions about whether he can comfortably fit into the Mayaro setting. This question can be interpreted on two levels. Firstly, the Caribbean writers and intellectuals, who are educated in foreign countries, find it difficult to fit into the cultures and systems of their countries. Secondly, the Caribbean, after independence, faces new challenges about its future course of action, especially in the face of postcolonial corruption and compromise.

In *The Castle of My Skin*, change comes to the village, bringing with it fear and misunderstanding, and for the boy, the realization that his island home is no longer his castle. His castle is in his skin, and his skin is both his pride and his prison. G's new consciousness parallels the new consciousness that is taking place in the village. For the first time Pa questions the reason for Slime's dismissal, and his motives for organizing the "penny bank" (the savings and loans system for the poor workers). Trumper returns from America with a revolutionized political consciousness. He sees things differently. On the central question of 'what makes a man?' he now disagrees with Pa and G's mother, and advocates a Marxist philosophy. He opposes Mr. Slime and others, and points out their selfish, greedy motives for buying the land. In the final moments, before G's departure, Trumper awakens G's awareness of a larger world and the predicament of humanity.

When Hat is imprisoned, the boy narrator misses him. He says, "When Hat went to jail, part of me had died" (214), but three years later, when Hat is released, things have changed. The narrator has grown from a boy to a man. He is now eighteen years old, earning money, and smoking. He no longer needs Hat as his father figure, he thinks critically, and sees the characters differently. He says:

> I was fifteen when Hat went to jail and eighteen when he came out. A lot happened in those three years. I left school and I began working in the customs. I was no longer a boy. I was a man, earning money...three years in which I had grown up and looked critically at the people around me. I no longer wanted to be like Eddoes. He was so weak and thin, and I hadn't realized that he was so small. Titus Hoyt was stupid and boring, and not funny at all. Everything had changed. (213-214)

## Finding a Place to Call Home in the Mother Country

Many nations, races, cultures, tribes, and peoples are displaced, disrupted, and disinherited. They are troubled and confused, so they rage against each other and against different cultures, religions, races, and classes. At the core of the Middle East Crisis is that both Jews and Palestinians are deeply committed to finding and creating a home for themselves and their off-springs. On a global scale, these millions and more are really looking for a place they call home before they can discover and define themselves. They must find a place they can call home, from where they will map a path of freedom for themselves and others. And the religious and humanitarian responsibility is for people to help each other find homes. But before anyone can help others to find homes, they must first find their own homes, and be at peace with themselves and others. God wants humanity to find their homes first, and they can only be at home when God is at home in their hearts.

According to John McArthur, *Katoikeo* (dwell) is a compound word, formed from *kata* (down) and *oikeo* (to inhabit a house). In the context of this passage the connotation is not simply that of being inside the house of our **hearts,** but of being at home there, settled down as a family member. God cannot be "at home" in people's hearts until their inner person submits to the strengthening of His Spirit. Until the Spirit controls their lives, God cannot be comfortable there, but only stays like a tolerated visitor. Paul's teaching here does not relate to the *fact* of God's presence in the hearts of believers, but to the *quality* of His presence.

When God came with two angels to visit them, Abraham and Sarah immediately made preparations to entertain their guests in the best possible way. From the rest of the passage (Gen. 18) it is evident that Abraham and Sarah knew they were hosting God Himself. It is also evident that God felt at home with Abraham and Sarah. It seems significant that when, a short while later, God warned Lot to take his family and flee for their lives. He did not go Himself, but only sent the two angels (Gen. 19:1). Lot was a believer, but God did not feel at home in Lot's house as He did in Abraham's tent.

In his booklet *My Heart Christ's Home*, Robert Munger pictures the Christian life as a house, through which Jesus goes from room to room. In the library, which is the mind, Jesus finds trash and all sorts of worthless things, which He proceeds to throw out and replace with His Word. In the dining room of appetite He finds many sinful desires listed on a worldly menu. In the place of such things as prestige, materialism, and lust He puts humility, meekness, love, and all the other virtues for which believers are to hunger and thirst. He goes through the living room of fellowship, where He finds many worldly companions and activities, through the workshop, where only toys are being made, into the closet, where hidden sins are kept, and so on through the entire house. Only when He had cleaned every room, closet, and corner of sin and foolishness could He settle down and be at home.

Jesus enters the house of our hearts the moment He saves us, but He cannot live there in comfort and satisfaction until it is cleansed of sin and filled with His will. God is gracious beyond comprehension and infinitely patient. He continues to love those of His children who insist on spurning His will. But He cannot be happy or satisfied in such a heart. He cannot be fully at home until He is allowed to **dwell in** our **hearts** through the continuing **faith** that trusts Him to exercise His lordship over every aspect of our lives. How awesome and wonderful that the almighty—unique, incomparable, marvelous, great, loving, and holy God wants to live in our **hearts**, rule and gladdens our hearts, thrill and entertain our hearts, satisfy and envision our hearts, and be at home there!

"Where are you from? Where do you live? Or where do you work?" are some questions adults ask to consciously or unconsciously determine our social status in life. These questions or determinations become urgent and critically important to dominant groups—Caucasian Americans, Canadians, and Europeans—if minority groups—immigrants, and/or people of color—decide to work in their companies or move into their communities or suburbs. Youths are preoccupied with, "What school did/do you go to? What do your parents do?" or a little later, "Which college do/did you go to? Or where do you plan to work, or where are you working?" These questions are all part of a culture that seeks to compose a picture or profile of us; a profile consisting of family background, income, social status, intelligence, and personality; a profile that will determine the future of the relationship between the subject and the object.

The above religious analogy is appropriately used for England, who has been the champion of Christianity, especially during their colonial rule over more than two thirds of the then known world. This little, but important country was like Christ's representative on the earth, taking the light of the gospel to the "heart of darkness," but at the same time offering a cold and callous reception to the multitudes, who came from colonies underdeveloped by British colonization and/or riddled by racial and ethnic wars—a sort of reversed reception for "Colonization in Reverse." Phillip Mohabir questions the authenticity and sincerity of a sector of British Christianity:

> They[2] were cold shouldered when they went to churches or straightforwardly asked not to return as they were an embarrassment to the other members of the congregation . . . When they entered certain buildings for worship and sat down, some worshippers would either get up and move down the bench, or move to another row. At the end of the meeting, the pastor saying goodbye to everyone at the door would turn his back on them, as if to pretend they did not exist. And these [White Brits] were the same people who had sent missionaries to them [immigrants of color especially from the Caribbean]. (68)

Mohabir further explains his bewilderment: "It was bewildering and perplexing, to say the least. If they were good enough to belong to the same denomination in the West Indies, why were they not good enough to belong here?" (69). Deplorable living conditions and a lack of belonging and connection made this new home for many immigrants a "cardboard world" according to Christophine (Rhys).

My intention in this section is to demonstrate how British colonialism created conditions of lack and underdevelopment in her former colonies forcing massive migration of their natives to England, their mother country; and how these natives encountered cold and callous responses of racism from their mother country. Works referenced include: George Lamming's *Pleasures of Exile*, Samuel Selvon's *Lonely Londoners*, V S Naipaul's *The Mimic Men*, *Half a Life*, *Magic Seeds*, and *Enigma of Arrival*, Jean Rhys' *Voyage in the Dark* and *Wide Sargasso Sea*, Michele Cliff's *Abeng* and *No Telephone to Heaven*, Philip Mohabir's *Building Bridges*, and Caryl Phillips' *A Distant Shore*.

With the arrival of the Europeans in the New World, in this case the West Indies, the home of the indigenous people was disrupted. The coloniz-

ers, however, created for themselves a temporary tourist home in the Caribbean for capitalistic purposes, but their real homes remained elsewhere. Yet
the colonizers disrupted the homes, families, communities, and nations of Africa and Asia to bring cheap labor forces through slavery and indenture ser-
vantship. Thus Africans and Asians (mainly Indians) would spend centuries of
colonial rule recovering from their cultural, spiritual, and psychological up-
rootings and creating a new home in the Caribbean. But they were "no longer
at ease" under colonialism. Prospero had come to Caliban's islands and left
the Calibans and Ariels in the aftermath of genocide, slavery, indenture ser-
vantship, imprisonment, dependency, and inferiority. Having used the "divide
and rule" to conquer the natives, to destabilize freedom, to create moral, spiritual, economic, and cultural chaos, and to promote restlessness and homeless-
ness; the colonizers retreated to their homes. But the colonized were left
homeless in their new homelands.

Prewar and postwar crises provided opportunities for many of these West
Indians, like the Africans and Asians, to migrate for better opportunities at
recreating a new home abroad. Jean Rhys' *Voyage in the Dark* (1934) is "the
story of a girl from the islands adrift in a mean and savage city." Early in the
novel, the heroine tells us:

> This is London—hundreds thousands of white people rushing along and the dark
> houses all alike frowning down one after the other all alike and stuck together—the
> streets like smooth shut-in ravines and the dark houses frowning down—oh I'm not
> going to like this place I'm not going to like this place. (20)

By the mid 1970s major changes had taken place in the immigrant population. According to Kenneth Ramchand, Linton Kwesi Johnson's *Dread Beat
and Blood* (1975) "gave soulful expression to the longing and violence of a generation born in England of West Indian parents, with little knowledge or experience of the West Indies, and without an undisputed place in their new
homeland" (3). But by the early 21st century Caryl Phillips' *A Distant Shore*
(2003) states with irony and sarcasm, "England has changed" (1). The question
raised however, is how is England changed, and Richard Wright's response to
the race question in the United States of America in the 1950s becomes appropriate: "the manifestations of race question has changed, but the nature of
the problem remains the same" (*Black Boy*).

Between the prewar generation of *Voyage in the Dark* and the postwar gen-
eration of Black British of West Indian parentage, however, we have a flow of
West Indians in search of home in the mother country. R. B. Davison's *West
Indian Migrants* (1962) explains:

At the end of the war these men returned home to find a disappointing situation. Jobs were hard to find and the standard of living they could expect in their home islands was much lower than that which they had enjoyed in Britain. There were no restrictions on their entry into Britain, for their passports bore witness to the fact that they were "citizens of the United Kingdom and Colonies." They began to trickle back to Britain to seek their fortunes and began to write home glowing accounts (backed up by cash remittances) of the varied opportunities available in the booming post-war British economy. Shipping companies, sensing a new avenue for profit, began to offer cheap fares to Britain in vessels returning to Europe and migration developed rapidly. (35)

Jamaican Louise Bennett describes this state of affairs as "Colonisation in Reverse":

> By de hundred, by de t'ousan
> From country and from town
> By de ship-load, by de plane-load
> Jamaica is England boun.

Samuel Selvon's third person omniscient narrator in *The Lonely Londoners* supports Bennett: "it not like long time when forty or fifty straggling in, they invading the country by the hundreds" (24). By 1956 when *The Lonely Londoners* was published, the annual migrant figure from the West Indies was 25,000 (Ramchand 4). Socio-economic and political conditions in the Caribbean, a "diseased society,"[3] were getting harsher with the demands for independence from many British colonies.

Many West Indian migrants gave up their space and freedom, at home in the Caribbean, in pursuit of an illusive dream of a reversed El Dorado in England, their mother country. This was the reversed Atlantic Slave Trade of trickery and fraud. Once, the colonized were captured and brought as slaves or tricked and brought to the Caribbean as Indenture Servants, then they were lied to that they cannot governor themselves so they needed a colonial Master, now they were dazzled by the promise of a prosperous home in their mother country, England, working for their Queen. In reality though, this dream was not even "a dream deferred," but a nightmare. Ramchand claims that Selvon's immigrants inhabit a nightmare world" (8), and Selvon captures this nightmare in a scene at Waterloo Station with the bewildered Tolroy and his newly migrated mother and extended family:

A old woman who look like she dead any minute come out of a carriage, carrying a cardboard box and a paperbag. When she get out the train she stand up there on the platform as if she confuse. Then after she a young girl come, carrying a flourbag filled up with things. Then a young man wearing a widebrim hat and a jacket falling below the knees. Then a little boy and a little girl, then another old woman, tottering so much a guard had was to help she get out of the train.

"Oh Jesus Christ," Tolroy say, "what is this at all?"

"Tolroy," the first woman say, "you don't know you own mother?"

Tolroy hug his mother like a man in a daze, then he say: "But what Tanty Bessy doing here, ma? and Agnes and Lewis and the two children?"
"All of we come, Tolroy," ma say. (29)

Again at Waterloo, the omniscient narrator tells of Moses', the first person narrator's, nightmarish experience:

When he get to Waterloo he hop off and went in the station, and right away in that big station he had a feeling of homesickness that he never felt in the past nine-ten years he in this country. For the old Waterloo is a place of arrival and departure, is a place where you see people crying goodbye and kissing welcome, and he hardly have time to sit down on a bench before this feeling of nostalgia hit him and he was surprise. (25-26)

Selvon's London is similar to V. S. Naipaul's London as seen through the experience and narrative of Ralph Singh in *The Mimic Men* (1967).[4] Singh's shipwreck is due to England's colonization of Isabella, the fictional island of composite Guyana, Trinidad, and Jamaica, and London's dehumanization of West Indian, Asian, and African migrants, like Singh. He describes this paralysis of fragmentation and dislocation of people being "trapped into fixed postures," of "the personality divided bewilderingly into compartments," and of "the panic ceasing to feel myself as a whole person" (9). Selvon's third person omniscient narrative voice echoes this colonial crippling effect of London on its West Indian immigrants in search of a place call home:

It have people in London who don't know what happening in the room next to them, far more the street, or how other people living. London is a place like that. It divide up in little worlds, and you stay in the world you belong to and you don't know anything about what happening in the other ones except what you read in the papers. (74)

Eventually, these lonely Londoners' disease, dislocation, and disillusionment force them into madness, mimicry, and corruption (Ramchand 9), which climax Ralph Singh's final shipwreck. Similarly, "as intellectual history, *The Pleasures of Exile* (1960) is specific to the colonial Caribbean" (Paquet viii). Here Lamming records that he and Selvon "were always together," on the ship, "like members of some secret society" (212), but his [Lamming's] "pneumonia had given way to another fear," the fear of TB (212-13). From pneumonia to TB to "a nervous condition" at Waterloo: "At Waterloo the Boys started to get nervous again. The train had encouraged amnesia; but at last we were on solid ground. Most of us had no idea where we would be going from here; but the question remained: 'Where will John sleep?'" (218). A few years later than the arrival of Selvon, Lamming, and Naipaul in England, Philip Mohabir arrived in London, not as a writer, but as a teenager and missionary, and he records a similar illusion of home of the West Indian immigrants in *Building Bridges* (1988):

> Eventually the train pulled up, brakes screeched: Victoria Station. So, on 16th April 1956, I had arrived in London. The doors flung open and instantly people poured out onto the platform. It is difficult to describe the scene, with relatives and loved ones who had not seen each other for years suddenly shouting and embracing one another, some laughing, some weeping. The warmth and joy of the occasion can hardly be captured in words. I stood there alone with my suitcase, feeling rather out of it all. (49)

He continues, "I felt cold and bewildered"(50). Mohabir further describes the lostness, meaninglessness, and insignificance of the West Indians in Brixton:

> Since my arrival at Victoria I had not seen so many people of my own color in one place.... Disillusionment was written indelibly on many faces.... In spite of the intermingling, somehow there was no real sense of integration; they did not seem to belong. A people uprooted: a migrant minority, searching for a place in the sun, a home in a foreign country for a future.... These people were like sheep distressed, weary and downcast and without a shepherd. (61)

These writers have also noted the role of race and color complicating the immigrants' search for a home of meaning and significance. Mohabir tells how they had become "conscious of discrimination, racial prejudice, of being second class citizens, unwanted and not respected" (69). Galahad's attempt at reaching out to a child, who exclaims, "Mummy, look at that black man!" in *The Lonely Londoners*, turns into pathos and analysis: "'Lord, what it is we people do in this world that we have to suffer so? What it is we want that the white people and them find it so hard to give? A little work, a little food, a little place to sleep. We are not asking for the sun, or the moon. We only want to get by, we don't even want to get on'" (88). His analysis identifies the color black as the source of the problems:

> Colour, is you that is causing all this, you know. Why the hell you can't be blue, or red or green, if you can't be white? You know is you that cause a lot of misery in this world. Is not me, you know, is you! Look at you, you so black and innocent, and this time, so you causing misery all over the world. (88)

So if Caryl Phillips is saying England has changed, but not changed, then Naipaul thinks that these conditions are still present, and passages in *Half a Life* (2001) and *Magic Seeds* (2004) support this conviction. Through Mahatma Gandhi's influence, Willie Somerset Chandram's father—a Brahmin—defies the intercaste's marriage code by marrying a low caste woman, and they have two children, Willie and Sarojini. In the 1950s Willie, like Naipaul, goes to England to find himself and to belong, but like his predecessor Ralph Singh, Willie indulges in a promiscuous lifestyle, until he meets and marries Asa. The couple move to Asa's estate/farm in a Portuguese colony in Eastern Africa. Not at home in India, nor in England, nor in Africa, Willie, at age 41, goes to Berlin to live with his sister Sarojini, who has been married to a German Photographer. In *Magic Seeds*, Willie joins an underground movement in India in an attempt to free the lower castes. But several years in prison and seven years of revolutionary campaigns awaken him to the realization that the revolution "had nothing to do with the village people we said we were fighting for...[that] our ideas and words were more important than their lives and their ambitions for themselves" (275). Moreover, Willie feels himself further than ever "from his own history and...from the ideas of himself that might have come to him with that history" (276). But back in England, he comes to see himself as a man "serving an endless prison sentence" (278).

From these two more recent works by Naipaul, one sees fictional and Autobiographical connections. One also sees sincerity in the questioning of "Where do I belong? Where is my home? Will it ever be possible for the migrant West Indian to find his/her home at home and/or abroad?" For Naipaul, and many West Indians, real home may not be found, even in an "imaginary homeland" as Salman Rushdie explains about global transplantation (8). In fact, at age 76, Naipaul is still trying to address the question of finding home in post-independence, postcolonialism, postmodernism, and globalization. And if there is any indication of the investment of Naipaul's feelings into Willie, we have a major tragedy, a tragedy of a brilliant Nobel Laurette, who is displaced from India, the Caribbean, and even from England, a country he has called home.

In contrast to Naipaul, Derek Walcott sees the migrant traveling West Indian writer as a Prodigal, who after traveling the world and being enriched by global and multicultural experiences, returns to the Caribbean, searching for his home:

> The *Prodigal* is a journey through physical and mental landscapes, from Greenwich Village to the Alps, from Pescara to Milan, from Germany to Cartagena. But always in "the music of memory, water" abide St. Lucia, the author's birthplace, and the living sea.... Derek Walcott has created a sweeping yet intimate epic of an exhausted Europe studded with church spires and mountains, train stations and statuary, a place where the New World is an idea, a "wavering map," and where History subsumes the natural history of his "unimportantly beautiful" island home. Here, the wanderer fears that he has been tainted by his exile, that his life has become untranslatable, and that his

craft itself has been rooted in the betrayal of the vivid archipelago to which he must return for the sustenance of life. (Book Jacket)

Home, therefore, for the West Indians may take different roads and many more years to reach, but some, like Walcott, are beginning to experience home in different ways.

## The Significance of the 'Tenement Yard' in Caribbean Nationalism as Reflected in Caribbean Literature

The Caribbean offers a rich culture and experience which originate from two main sources. Firstly, the Caribbean comprises of several countries, with a mixture of people—the Amerindians, East Indians (people of Asian ancestry), Africans (people of African ancestry), Chinese, Europeans, Americans, Mulattoes, and Douglas (a fast growing population; mixed-race people of African and Indian ancestries). Secondly, the history of the Caribbean. Each country has its own unique history, and yet they share a common past. On one hand, the Caribbean shares the common experience of slavery, indentureship, colonialism, and economic depravity. On the other hand, each country is unique in that each country, colonized by either England, Holland, Spain, France, or Portugal, has changed hands of ownership several times before its independence. These differences are present in the people's culture.

Against this multicultural background in a postcolonial setting, several Caribbean writers have written literary pieces as explorations of the experiences of the Caribbean. One aspect of this experience is 'Tenement Yard Drama.' This aspect is present in V.S. Naipaul's work, *Miguel Street*, where the street becomes a metaphor for not only Trinidad, but also for the entire Caribbean. Similarly, *The Rose Ship* by Douglas Archibald and *Moon on a Rainbow Shawl* by Errol John are fine examples of plays, which explore the theme, 'Tenement Yard Drama.' This section of chapter three focuses on 'Tenement Yard Drama in *Moon on a Rainbow Shawl*.'

The setting of this play is Trinidad, in the back yard property of Old Mack, in the East Dry River district. There are two dilapidated buildings in the yard. In one building Adams and Rosa occupy the two apartments. In the other, Ephraim and Mavis occupy the two apartments. The living conditions are deplorable, and Old Mack, the landlord, shows no sign of bettering the housing facilities. In the center of the yard is the stand pipe.

It is within the confines of such a yard that people live. They love, hate, quarrel, sing and express their frustrations from day to day. The tension of living under such poor economic and social condition is so high that Sophia "throws words at Mavis," while Mavis "throws stones at Sophia." Prince and the American Solider fight. Sophia "lashes Charlie with her tongue," and Ephraim fights to escape the viciousness of a society that traps him. Rosa cannot understand why the people quarrel so much, but Ephraim gives her the reason.

> Rosa:  Why they have to quarrel so?
> Eph:   To ease the tension.
> Rosa:  What tension?
> Eph:   Of livin' like hogs.

Indeed "livin' like hogs" is what makes it tenement yard drama, and the yard becomes a metaphor for Trinidad and the entire Caribbean. It is also a metaphor for the millions of exploited and marginalized people around the globe, as well as for the condition of millions of Black South Africans under apartheid in townships like Soweto.

A cat, who is generally timid, will shy away from strangers. He escapes from dangers, but if locked in a room and attacked, his survival is threatened. He feels trapped and insecure. He will strike back at his attackers. This is precisely the point Richard Wright makes in his runaway bestseller, *Native Son*, which opens with the rat scene—a foreshadowing of Bigger Thomas' world of fear, imprisonment, and violence. It is also the world of hundreds of thousands of poor African Americans living in the Black Belt (Chicago's Southside in the early 20th century). The feeling of being trapped is probably the strongest features of the tenement yards.

In this yard of *Moon on a Rainbow Shawl*, the characters are part of a vicious cycle, which traps them and offers them a certain amount of hopelessness. Rosa is a product of such a system. She is an orphan, insecure and in need of love. She finds it, to some extent, in Sophia. She works at Old Mack's café, and her world suddenly brightens in her love affair with Ephraim. However, she blunders by accepting Old Mack's favors (such as driving her home and giving her material things e.g. earrings, shoes, dresses, chains, watches, etc.), and by not ensuring that Ephraim knows earlier that she is pregnant for him. She blunders to a man who is also trapped and insecure, and she loses her chance of a continued relationship with Ephraim, who tells her: "Even up to this minute gone, I wasn't sure in my mind. I say things work out for me, I SEND FER YER! But from now on, girl, yer sweet old man alone will have to do ..." (52).

This innocent, naïve, orphan girl, in a desperate fight against insecurity, realizes that Ephraim is not going to marry her. She is thrown out and like the cat's fight for survival, she fights back. Crying out, Rosa turns beating at Ephraim with her fists and utters the most astonishing words: "Yer is a damn worthless nigger! Yer mother walk out on you! You kill yer own grand-mother! ..." (55). By this time Ephraim lifts her off the ground and literally throws the girl out of his room, hurling her dress, shoes, and shawl after her. Rosa continues:

> Do you think! Do you think I want a man like you to marry me and father my child? You go! You go wherever the hell you wants to go! And when the time come for yer to dead, I hope yer dead like the bastard you are, yer two foot stick up high in the air. (55)

Rosa is disillusioned. Her moon or dream is shattered. Her rainbow is gone, and the reality of surviving with a child, in the yard, drives her to inten-sify her relationship with Old Mack—a symbol of patriarchal and neocolonial exploiter. Therefore, at the end of the play, when Ephraim leaves for Liver-pool, it is disappointing, but not surprising to hear Old Mack calling for Rosa, from Rosa's room. She escapes into Old Mack's material world for security. Sophia, Rosa's surrogate mother, realizes the depravity of Rosa's situation and exclaims, "O God! No!" (85), but Sophia can do nothing because she is help-less since she is also trapped in the yard.

Sophia Adams, in her late thirties, but the hard conditions have made her to appear older, is the backbone of her family. She is the strong mother figure, with which so much of Caribbean literature is occupied. She labors, as a do-mestic, to provide for her family, and her dream is to get out of the yard: "I pray for the day Charlie start working steady, so we could get out of all this" (38). Getting out of the tenement yard, however, is difficult since she too is trapped. Ephraim reminds her: "To get out! That's the thing! Yer have to stay here, Living like this, Is as if yer trapped" (38).

Sophia, like the others from the yard, dreams of a brighter day, a happier life, a house of her own in a more habitable environment. But her dream is also shattered when her husband, Charlie, is "strangled by the big ones". Sophia longs to escape from the yard, or just run away at times. She tells Eph-raim, "Run all yer! Run boys! Run! Sometimes I wish I could do a little run-ning myself" (42). Nevertheless, her strong faith and courage, which are inspired by her religion, keep her stable and strong. She still has a thin hope for a brighter future. This hope is in the possible consistent employment of Charlie and the education of Esther.

Can Charlie provide this deliverance for his family from the yard? It is clear that Charlie's ambitious resistance is low, his dream is shattered, and in total disillusionment he escapes into drunkenness. Charlie becomes the most pathetic figure in the play. Rosa looks at him as if she has seen a ghost and

Sophia bullies him and whips him, verbally. When he stays out all night, the frustrated Sophia tells her daughter, Esther: "I trying mey best. Since seven 'clock this morning I up to mey elbows in that damn wash tub. He going get such a tongue lashing from me this mornin" (30).

In act three, scene one, when Sophia breaks the news of Charlie's theft and imprisonment to Esther, the girl accuses her mother of causing Charlie's dilemma: "Is you! Is you! If Daddy did what you say he did! Is you! Always pushing him and pushing him. And making him feel shame in front of all kinds of people. Is you! Is you! Is you! (77).

Charlie's only hope lies in Esther. This is why he steals seventy dollars, from Old Mack's café, to purchase personal necessities for Esther to take up the scholarship. He is disillusioned and is stripped of his authority by a system filled with discriminations. With a promising career in cricket, a major sport in the Caribbean, Charlie's future is "strangled by the Big Ones." The reason is because he radically points out the discrimination of the hotel accommodation system. He is never selected again for the cricket team, and he loses his chance of playing English County Cricket. He now drinks, stays away from home, and prepares bats as a part-time job.

Mavis has resorted to prostitution as her mode of living. Constantly, there is the sound of passionate lustful laughter, musical revelry, and the rhythm of abusive language. There are also dramatic scenes of fight and confrontation. These are all attributes of the tenement yard drama. For example, as Mavis brings in another client, an American soldier, she leaves Joe a while, comes down the steps, picks up a stone, and throws it against the shutters of the Adams' door. Sophia turns on the light and appears at the door:

Sophia:  Woman! Is the damn fool yer playin' nah?
Mavis:   Peeping, peeping, peeping! I wish the blasted stone did lick out yer eye!
Sophia:  B'Jesus Christ! It would have been me an' you tonight! I would of cut yer to pieces like a mad dog, yer damn little whore!
Mavis:   Yer mother was the first one!
Sophia:  And your mother before she! (46)

Mavis again provides a bawdy scene, when Prince, her regular boyfriend and later her husband, discovers the American Soldier in Mavis' room, he starts a fight with the soldier. As they crash into Mavis' room, she runs out shouting, "O God! Prince, the Yankee goin' kill yer! Don't hit him! Yer can't fight, Prince, yer know yer can't fight" (54).

She runs out into the yard and continues, "He can't fight. Ever since yer had your hernia yer can't fight. Don't hit him! Don't hit him! Murder! Murder! POLICE! MURDER!" (59). This is Mavis' world. The world she has escaped into, and although Sophia rejects Mavis' world by trying to get her out of the yard or by escaping herself, it will be a long time before any of them truly escape. Mavis is married to Prince, but one suspects she will continue her trade: Eph: (speaking to Prince as he eases himself out of Mavis' embrace) I see yer. Mavis: Anytime! Right now, if you like! So tonight, if yer go! I sure it will bring yer back!" (72).

Ephraim would not be seduced by the fleeting pleasures of Mavis' body since he recognizes that they are all trapped, and his way of escape is to immigrate to Liverpool. At age five, his father dies, at six his mother runs off with another man; and he is left hungry when he is rescued by his grandmother. Later, the grandmother becomes an obstacle to his escape, so he puts her in a poor house, and shortly after she dies. Ephraim is not cruel or callous, but terribly insecure. He fears being hindered from escaping from the yard. Throughout the play he is compassionate, caring, and tender. He cares for Esther, the baby, and Charlie. He loves Rosa, but informed at the wrong time and under suspicious circumstances about Rosa's pregnancy, his insecurity can only conclude one motive, the motive to trap him.

> Rosa:  I'm pregnant.
> *There is a pause.*
> Eph:  Pregnant?
> Rosa:  Yes.
> Eph:  Fer who?
> Rosa:  (smiling) Eph!
> Eph:  This is no joke.
> Rosa:  Fer you.
> Eph:  Make me laugh.
> Rosa:  Fer you Ephraim.
> Eph:  Trap
> Rosa:  No.
> Eph:  (wildly) TRAP! Who the hell yer think yer talking to? TRAP! Go
> tell yer ole man that! (53)

Ephraim's insight into the viciousness of the society, that does not develop the people, helps him to see Charlie's problem, and he uses situations like that of Charlie and old Sam to further resolve to leave the Caribbean:

> Trouble with Charlie, he was a dreamer and old as he is he ent loss that dream yet. But I'm young and I'm wide awake. And it ent my intention to remain here and grow a big white moustache like Ole Sam, who used to drive tramcar, and when the trolley's come, they pension him off with a pittance. (41)

Ephraim sees his job as a dehumanizing one. One that gets you no where, except going around in a circle. He says of his job: "Eight hours a day, up

Henry Street, down Park Street, Tragarette Road, St. James Terminus, Turn it around! Back down town again! And around again! O Lord!" (20).

Esther, Rosa, and Sophia feel that Ephraim is going to be able to break away from the 'yard' because he will be promoted to Inspector, so he should stay. But he reminds Esther that Inspectors have to ride on the trolleys too, then he explodes to Rosa:

> I got one life to live! Awright! So I stay here. I come an Inspector on the trolley. To what end? Turn maco like the rest. Stand at a bus stop. Hop on the trolley, check the ticket. Hop off the trolley! To what end, Rosa? Just so as to see the conductors don't rob the blasted city corporation. (54)

In the last scene, in the final attempt to stay Ephraim, Sophia tries to prevent him from leaving, but Ephraim is not going to be stopped. He would listen to Sophia, the strong mother-figure of the yard, but not now. In a burst of desperation, as he runs out to the taxi, he shouts: "TAKE ME OUT OF THIS BLASTED PLACE! GO! GO!! GO!!!" (84).

The yard, a microcosm of the Caribbean, not only traps the characters, frustrates their dreams, fills them with disillusionment, and forces them into escapes and escapism; but also exploits them. Old Mack, the Landlord, represents the slave masters, colonizers, exploiting capitalists, and the European planters in absenteeism. The conditions of the houses and surroundings are deplorable, yet Old Mack collects his monthly rent, but never bothers to repair the buildings or the domestic facilities. Instead, he is constructing a steal and concrete three story building, which "dominates, like some tall phantom, the two lowly dwellings in the yard" (14).

When Sophia learns of the robbery at Old Mack's café, she rejoices:

> Thief from thief child, does make Jehovah laugh! And I is only a mere mortal. It serve him right. The way he robbing we here with the rent on these nasty little rooms. Serve him right. Every darn night. Somebody should go in there and carry way something. (32)

A little later Ephraim, pointing to the unfinished structure in the yard, tells Sophia:

> All that waste. The blasted ole fool. He's got a house. Yet he starts putting that up. Three stories high. To live in! Himself alone. Now is months since a workman was here. Don't you think Mrs. Adams, that instead of Old Mack wastin' time and money on a thing like that! Don't you think he could of build a decent kitchen fer you? Fix up the bathroom? Put on a roof? Use some paint back here? (39)

Old Mack goes further in his exploitation by exploiting Rosa. He uses the trick of buying gifts for her. He gives her watches, rings, chains, shoes, dresses, etc, drives her home, and gives her any off-day with pay. Although, at first, "like a Baptist preacher giving baptism" (25), he fails to obtain sexual favors from Rosa, later he is in Rosa's house, not only as the landlord, but as the "man of the house."

Is there any hope for the people of this tenement yard? The image of the rainbow represents their quest for fulfillment. Each is looking for a brighter day ahead, for the Promised Land, for a better yard. They are all striving to get out of the low social and economic conditions, to get to the moon or the rainbow, but can they reach the rainbow, which is just an illusion?

Ephraim would seem to be the main hope, but this is not so. He is careful and illusive as the rainbow. Immigrating to England is going into another vicious circle of life. It is probably worse than the trolley bus driver in Trinidad, since he will spend the years ahead dealing with loss of identity, fragmentation, loneliness, displacement and alienation. These are other tenement yard conditions in an illusively glorified manner in London as described in Samuel Selvon's *The Lonely Londoners*. In spite of prevailing frustration and disillusionment, however, there is hope. The hope lies in Esther. Esther is a key figure, who represents a real life promise. Her education is seen as a way out of poverty, and the characters want Esther to succeed.

Esther is also a biblical name. In the *Bible*, Esther is a Jewish heroine who becomes Queen to Xerxes, the Persian King, and because of the King's favor towards her, she is able to save her people from destruction planned by the wicked Haman (Esther). Esther, is seen as the one who will go away on the Island Scholarship, study and come back to help her people out of the tenement yard drama. Ephraim tells her:

> Yer know, Esther. When yer grow up, It would be kind of nice if yer could go away and study, on an Island Scholarship or something. Come back, Big! Yer know! Make everybody respect yer. (20)

# Notes

1. These points are presented here as broad stories to highlight the canon of Caribbean literature, but in chapter seven they are elaborated as part of the experiment of alienation producing madness.

2. These were people of color, mainly West Indians, in Brixton. Mohabir describes them as "thousands of people needing help—homeless, discouraged, unemployed, disillusioned people: people whose dreams were shattered, who could not cope with the cold weather, who were separated from family and friends. They had started to arrive during the war, recruited as soldiers to fight for their King and country. Later, they were invited to take up certain jobs in hospitals, factories and transport services, especially in the post-war years, the early fifties" (67). These were jobs others would not take.

3. Albert Memmi calls a colonized society a disease society.

4. It should be noted that Samuel Selvon, George Lamming, and V. S. Naipaul came to England in the same year, 1950. Selvon and Lamming came on the same ship.

# CHAPTER FOUR

# Multicultural and Postcolonial Interpretations of Caribbean Literature and Its Environment

The nineteenth century, from a colonial perspective, is seen as a period of historical adventurism, a period of world exploration from which emerged numerous travelogues, diaries, letters, and reports describing, in a mysterious and exotic manner, the land and people of the new world. Whether these conquistadors were Spanish, British, French, Dutch, or Portuguese, they were primarily white Europeans who were curiously intrigued and fascinated by what they perceived as the dark worlds of Asians, Indians, and Africans. Within this periodic frame, writers like Joseph Conrad, Graham Greene, Rudyard Kipling, Coral Ballantyne, and others, motivated and influenced by these expedition stories, sailed to many of these new regions and wrote voraciously about the peoples and their landscapes. Dictated by the hunger, thirst, and even lust for exotic descriptions and mysterious narratives from the European audience, these writers' works merely reinforced the myths and legends previously depicted by the colonizers. For example, Conrad's depiction of Africa as evil and Africans as savages. According to Achebe, Conrad's "*Heart of Darkness* projects the image of Africa as 'the other world,' the antithesis of Europe and therefore of civilization, a place where man's vaunted intelligence and refinement are finally mocked by triumphant bestiality" (252).

Later, another group of writers such as E. M. Forester and H. G. de Lisser would build on such dehumanizing depictions, devaluing the colonized and their environment. H. G. de Lisser, for example, one of the earliest Caribbean writers, "after giving an unnaturally happy ending to the realistic portrait of a poor servant girl in *Jane's Career: A Story of Jamaica* (1914), increasingly turned to exotic historical novels about pirates, witchcraft and romantic love" (King, Introduction 2). Homi Bhabha, in "Representation in the Colonial Text," sums up the effects of the former and latter's colonial representation in the following manner:

> In shattering the mirror of representation, and its range of Western bourgeois social and psychic "identifications," the spectacle of colonial fantasy sets itself as an uncanny "double." Its terrifying figures—savages, grotesques, mimicmen—reveal things so profoundly familiar to the West that it cannot bear to remember them. It is in that sense, and for that very reason, that "the horror! the horror!" said in the heart of darkness itself, and the "Ou-boum" of the empty Marabar caves will continue to terrify and confound us, for they address that "other scene" within ourselves that continually divides us against ourselves and others. (119-20)

It was not until the beginning of the latter half of the twentieth century that a recognizable body of literature began to emerge from the Caribbean, and this body of literature had the magnanimous task of debunking the colonial myth of negativity of the Caribbean land and its peoples. It also had to forge a pioneering path of discovery and definition against the onslaught of both black and white American criticism. Emerging from rumor and legend of "sailors, saltfish merchants, displaced criminals, yellow-fever victims, slaves in the canefields, Maroons in the bush," "the men and women who laid the foundations of Caribbean societies in the sixteenth and seventeenth centuries" (Dance 1), Caribbean literature was viewed as cheap and low-class. But after half of a century of focusing on neglected subjects like ordinary people, landscape, and environment, this region has produced several excellent writers of international renown and two literature Nobel laureates—Derek Walcott (1992) and V. S. Naipaul (2001).

Although most of the writers from the Caribbean had the opportunity to either live in or visit another country, namely England and later United States of America and Canada, their memories of the Caribbean environment and its peoples remained freshly intact. Whether writing from England, United States of America, Canada, or the Caribbean, these writers use the rich, tropical landscape of the Caribbean as setting and the socio-political and historical struggles as major themes. As a result, much of Caribbean literature explores the importance of belonging to a place, and when the feeling of belonging is destroyed, a person's identity crumbles. One can understand the writers' dilemma since most of them emerged in the forties and fifties, when a great wave of migration occurred. Living in foreign countries, Caribbean writers experienced alienation and displacement, and their experiences filter into their writings, consciously or unconsciously. For the most part, it is done consciously since literature becomes a means of evaluating and re-evaluating not only their homelands, but also themselves. While the narrators of *Miguel Street* and *In the Castle of My Skin* are reflective and analytical about their departure from the Caribbean, Moses and Ralph Singh, through story telling, oral and written, re-evaluate their shipwrecked lives in England. And these narrators reflect the nostalgia and self-analysis of the authors.

Displacement results from the historical and cultural struggles of the region. The occupation of various areas of the region at different periods by the Spanish, Dutch, French, and British has left much historical fragmentation. In his 1983 introduction to *In the Castle of My Skin*, Lamming indicated that British colonialism had created a fragmented society:

> It was not a physical cruelty. Indeed, the colonial experience of my generation was almost wholly without violence. No torture, no concentration camp, no mysterious disappearance of hostile natives, no army encamped with orders to kill. The Caribbean endured a different kind of subjugation. It was a terror of the mind; a daily exercise in self-mutilation. Black versus Black in a battle for self-improvement. (xiii)

Earl Lovelace's novel *The Schoolmaster* employs a consistent third-person narrative to demonstrate the colonial rupture caused to the traditional society by the encroaching modern society. Harold Bascom's use of a consistent third-person narrative in his novel *Apata* illustrates this idea. Lamming, however, *In the Castle of My Skin*, demonstrates that a single narrative technique is inadequate to illustrate the colonial fracture. Lamming points out in his introduction:

> The result was a fractured consciousness, a deep split in its sensibility which now raised difficult problems of language and values; the whole issue of cultural allegiance between imposed norms of White Power, represented by a small numerical minority, and the fragmented memory of the African masses: between white instruction and Black imagination. (xi)

The practice of slavery and indentureship has further complicated the wholeness of the region. Additionally, since most of these writers lived or live in foreign countries and experienced or experience alienation, loneliness, and loss of culture, their writings reflect this displacement. Rochester is very much displaced in the Caribbean as Antoinette is in England. The West Indians in England, as described by Samuel Selvon's *The Lonely Londoners*, experience displacement. They lose themselves, their culture, environment, and their sense of community. Although Moses tries to revive and foster the community spirit, by allowing fellow West Indians to meet, eat, and sleep at his apartment, the community still disintegrates because of the absence of their environment.

This is one of the inevitable consequences they suffer for living in a foreign, large city. Thus, they become fragmented, and out of fragmentation they live crippled lives. But their nostalgia for their warm, beautiful islands juxtaposed with a cold, frigid England forges a self-analysis that parallels re-evaluation from the first wave of migrated Caribbean writers. Moses, the narrator and contemplated writer, reflects:

> I does wonder about the boys, how all of we come up to the old Brit'n to make a living, and how the years go by and we still here in this country.... How after all these years I ain't get no place at all, I still the same way, neither forward nor backward.... From winter to winter, summer to summer, work after work. Sleep, eat, hustle pussy, work, Boy, sometimes I sit there and think about that.... I want to go back to Trinidad and lay down in the sun and dig my toes, and eat a fish broth and go Maracas Bay and talk to them fishermen, and all day long I sleeping under a tree, with just the old sun for company. (Selvon, *The Lonely Londoners* 129–30)

Selvon—of Indian father and Indian/Scottish mother—grew up in Trinidad's multi-racial society. With such perspective, he explores the fractured and displaced migrant community in England through fiction. The characters of his novels, especially *The Lonely Londoners*, *Moses Ascending* (1975), and *Moses Migrating* (1984) seek to recreate their lost Caribbean multicultural community of belongingness.

Jean Rhys left the Caribbean at age 17 (1907) and returned once (1936) before publishing *Wide Sargasso Sea* in 1966. Yet the vividness of memory of and the sharpness of nostalgia for the Caribbean environment and the people punctuate the novel with multicultural and postcolonial themes and concerns before these became major bodies of critical investigation. Antoinette desperately tries to escape from the negation of her life, to assert her individual identity. She tries to answer the parrot's questions, "Who's there? Who are you?" (41). But her quest for identity encounters patriarchal domination, and in some ways her plight reflects a similar fate of the Caribbean because of the cultural and political domination from metropolitan countries. Through the loss of a sense of place or the failure to identify with the Caribbean landscape, her identity is destroyed. Antoinette loves the Caribbean, especially Coulibri and Dominica, but due to patriarchal and colonial interference from Mason and Rochester, she is uprooted from both places. Of course Mason's marriage to Annette is central to the riot at Coulibri, the parallel of Eden (19), and this riot drives the family from their fallen paradise. Antoinette's effort to remain at Coulibri is thwarted by a "jagged stone" from Tia. However, she clings to this place: "As I ran, I thought, I will live with Tia and I will be like her. Not to leave Coulibri. Not to go. Not" (45). Later, in brooding nostalgia, she tells Rochester about the intensity of her love for Dominica and Coulibri: "'I love it [Dominica] more than anywhere in the world. As if it were a person.' 'But you don't know the world,' I teased her. 'No, only here, and Jamaica of course. Coulibri Spanish Town'" (89).

Colonial and postcolonial Caribbean writers have depicted their land and environment in a reverential, personified, and intimate manner—a harmonious and symbolic setting for their characters and actions. This personification creates a rather complex and interesting mosaic relationship between the peoples and their landscapes. On one level, the colonizer 'rapes' the land, sets out to conquer violently the environment, and encounters hostile resistance. He uses his social, political, and economic authority/power to condemn the landscape as evil and destructive. Whereas the colonized respects the land and environment, celebrates their energy and beauty, and draws strength from their fountains of life. Antoinette is strong and passionate in the Caribbean landscape, which consists of hot sun, green vegetation, and fresh running streams. She is in harmony with this colorful landscape, which contains her "tree of life," thereby supplying her with life (19). Antoinette colors her roses in green, blue, and purple, and writes her name in "fire red" (53). But for the wounded and fragmented Rochester, "everything is too much.... Too much blue, too much purple, too much green. The flowers are too red, the mountains are too high, the hills too near. And the woman is a stranger" (70). His failure to control and dominate the landscape renders him powerless: "I wanted to say something reassuring but the scent of the river flowers was overpoweringly strong. I felt giddy" (83), but it also symbolizes his inability to celebrate the colorful and passionate personality and sexuality of his wife. Threatened and terrified by the landscape, a fearful Rochester "broke a spray off and trampled it into the mud" (99), and his cold and callous way of destroying the landscape symbolizes the way he destroys Antoinette in order to control her. His greedy thirst/lust cannot be satisfied because his colonial perspective associates his hatred for Antoinette and her landscape:

> I hated the mountains and the hills, the rivers and the rain. I hated the sunsets of whatever color, I hated its beauty and its magic and the secret I would never know. I hated its indifference and the cruelty which was part of its loveliness. Above all I hated her. For she belonged to the magic and the loveliness. She had left me thirsty and all my life would be thirst and longing for what I had lost before I found it. (172)

This heavenly place where Antoinette belongs and where she wishes to stay (108), has been made into a hell by Rochester: "But I loved this place and you have made it into a place I hate. I used to think that if everything else went out of my life I would still have this, and now you have spoilt it. It's just somewhere else where I have been unhappy, and the other things are nothing to what has happened here" (147). Angier describes the implication of this destruction. She points out that "in destroying this place for Antoinette, Rochester precipitates her madness because he has destroyed her sense of hope, of belonging, of ownership, autonomy, and ultimately her own sense of personal power" (154). The magnitude of Antoinette's destruction forces her confession to her destroyer: "I hate it now like I hate you and before I die I will show you how much I hate you" (147).

In similar manner, Rochester, Mr. Mason, and other colonialists and colonizers respond negatively to the people of the Caribbean, a place Walcott describes as a sweet smelling and refreshing land made up of pieces from all other lands and peoples:

> Break a vase, and the love that reassembles the fragments is stronger than that love which took its symmetry for granted when it was whole. The glue that fits the pieces is the sealing of its original shape. It is such a love that reassembles our African and Asiatic fragments, the cracked heirlooms whose restoration shows its white scars. This gathering of broken pieces is the care and pain of the Antilles, and if the pieces are disparate, ill-fitting, they contain more pain than their original sculpture, those icons and sacred vessels taken for granted in their ancestral places. Antillean art is this restoration of our shattered histories, our shards of vocabulary, our archipelago becoming a synonym for pieces broken off from the original continent. (Nobel Speech 28)

Mr. Mason still sees the people of African descent as slaves or as inhuman. He underestimates their power of resistance, and therefore places himself and family in no position to prevent the Coulibri fire and the family's tragedy. Further, he calls them "niggers" and "Negroes," and believes that they are "too damn lazy to be dangerous" (32). Mr. Mason alienates Antoinette from her multiracial cousins (50), and, I strongly believe that, he hurriedly arranges for her marriage with Rochester in order to prevent her teenage relationship with Sandi (50, 58-59, 125). Rochester also, like those who came before him, can only relate to the peoples of the Caribbean as master to slaves/servants. His sexual relationship with Amelie is driven by revenge and control (140), and he has distaste for the people. He finds Christophine's language "horrible," and misunderstands and condemns the way the women wear their dresses for cultural observations (85). In his quest to conquer the Caribbean landscape and Antoinette, he has to get rid of the people who provide strength and life for Antoinette, and these people are from the multiracial community—namely Christophine and Sandi.

Derek Walcott, a reflection of Caribbean multiculturalism, uses his "schizophrenic" culture as a metaphor for Caribbean heterogeneity ("What the Twilight Says" 4). One of the recurring themes of Walcott's works is "the multicultural mixture of identities" (http://www.kirjasto.sci.fi/walcott.htm), which has emerged from his mixed heritage of African, British, and Dutch (Gaster). In *A Far Cry from Africa*, the painter and poet cry out:

> "I who am poisoned with the blood of both
> Where shall I turn, divided to the vein?
> I who have cursed
> The drunken officer of British rule, how choose
> Between this Africa and the English tongue I love?" (*A Far Cry from Africa*, 17–18)

Walcott further expresses the agony and beauty of his multiculturalism: "Mongrel as I am, something prickles in me when I see the word Ashanti as with the word Warwickshire, both separately intimating my grandfathers' roots, both baptizing this neither proud nor ashamed bastard, this hybrid, this West Indian" (Walcott, "The Muse of History" 20). As early as 1973 Derek Walcott fused his life and the Caribbean in *Another Life*, where he talks about the task of setting down the landscape and naming it. Walcott nostalgically recreates the Caribbean landscape, particularly St. Lucia, with the rich congruence of painting imageries, figures, and theories. *Another Life* opens with the young artist (Walcott) striving to sketch the landscape at sunset and ends with the maturing writer, Walcott. The journey-motif becomes a vehicle for the poet's exploration of the beauty and fire of St. Lucia, coconut walks of his father's paintings, history and oppression, freedom and romance, his beloved Andreuille who lives at the water's edge, Simmons and his studio, privilege and aspiration, and frustration and fulfillment. This autobiographical poem also describes, celebrates, and re-evaluates Walcott's life, art, love, landscape, language, history, the Caribbean, struggles of a few people, and spiritual resilience present in the human heart. Walcott looks at the standard view of Caribbean history and sees that colonization has depicted a distorted history filled with numerous gaps. In telling Caribbean history, the absence of facts renders the story as the hollowness of a coconut shell, thus, his intention is to provide autobiography, which he decorates with art and love, as an alternative to history, the accumulation of dead facts or the writing of a juiceless grocery list. Through autobiography, Walcott aims at the whole truth, which is multifaceted, and in the poem, he transmits his personal experience into art, providing an artistic vision and form through a synthesis of writing and painting.

Novelist, poet, and critic Wilson Harris, a trained government surveyor, is of "mixed European, African and Amerindian ancestry" (Maes-Jelinek 179). Additionally, he is from Guyana, the land of many waters and many races. Maes-Jelinek defines the two major elements that have shaped thinking of Harris' works: "the impressive contrasts of the Guyanese landscapes...and the successive waves of conquest which gave Guyana its heterogeneous population" (179). According to Boxill, Harris draws upon his "close experiences with nature and landscape, and with the men of different races and classes who were his surveying crews and who were isolated with him in the jungle or on riverbanks for considerable periods of time" (187-88). Further, Harris' travels from Guyana to England and North America become a movement of re-evaluation in time and space of his own relationship to the land and landscape he revisits in the settings of his works. Maes-Jelinek divides Harris' works into three major phases: "a composite picture of the many facets of Guyanese Life: the paradoxes and unpredictable manifestations of a nature that is not easily mastered, the historical vestiges, visible and invisible, that give each area a specific 'spirit of the place,' and the activities of a multiracial population often self-divided and alienated from its 'lost' or unintegrated groups such as the Amerindians or the descendants of runaway slaves" (183). His most famous work, *Palace of the Peacock*, depicts Donne, captain of a multiracial crew, as the colonizer who is obsessed with the conquest of the legendary El Dorado, the lost city of gold. His lust for gold parallels his lust for Mariella, the Amerindian woman, who harmonizes with the land and landscape, to destroy not only the process of colonization, but also the colonizer and his crew. Hena Maes-Jelinek argues that:

> not only do the outer and inner psychological landscapes coincide and real landscape features spatialize inner states of mind, the concrete and the intangible often overlap as again and again the surface reality is breached to reveal the tormenting obsessions of the crew with power or wealth, with Mariella, the native woman (at once sexual object, symbol of the land and the spirit of the place, and ambivalent muse), to reveal also the mixture of terror and beauty they experience in their journey towards death and rebirth. (450)

In fact, Wilson Harris is the only West Indian author who has devoted much of his work to an elevating representation of native West Indians/Indians/Amerindians, who are closest to the land and environment. H. G. de Lisser's *The Arawak Girl*, Edgar Mittleholzer's *Kaywana Trilogy* (*Kaywana Blood, Kaywana Stock, and Kaywana Children*), and Michael Gilkes' *Couvade* are three of the few authors who include the Amerindians in their works. Since the colonizers/Europeans "virtually eliminated" the natives, "the small communities which survive in Dominica and Guyana today are regarded as marginal to the society," and for this reason the little fiction in which they appear "either registers them as de-tribalised individuals in the towns ("Bucks") or portrays them as exotic groups in the interior" (Ramchand, "Aboriginies" 51). But Harris' works, particularly *Palace of the Peacock* and *Heartland*, place the Indians at the center of colonial, postcolonial, and multicultural representations of the land and the peoples' relationships to their environment. According to Ramchand, Harris places Indians at the center of "three of his basic themes in fiction: the unity of all men, the theme of rebirth, and the search for ancestral roots. At the same time, the author from Guyana makes the 'historical' Indian come alive in a way that no other West Indian novelist or historian has been bold enough to imagine" ("Aboriginies" 51).

The Guyanese land and landscape function like the gods in Greek literature to defend the poor and oppressed, the vanishing Amerindians in *Palace of the Peacock*, the poor East Indian laborers in *The Far Journey of Oudin*, and the descendants of runaway slaves in *The Secret Ladder*, and destroy the oppressors, namely the Europeans. Jungle and river falls in particular become ravenous wolves ready to devour the colonizers. Skipper Donne in *The Palace of the Peacock* travels up an unnamed river in the jungle of Guyana in pursuit of the Amerindian tribe for a kind of slave-labor, in order to build his empire, but he also pursues Mariella to rape, pillage, and plunder her. He has already physically and psychologically abused and exploited her as he has also done to the land. This conquer-and-control relationship Donne has with Mariella is symbolic of the relationship between the colonizer and the colonized. Further, through the use of history and myths and legends from the Amerindians, Harris' *Palace of the Peacock* "recreates quintessentially the repeated invasion of Guyana after the Renaissance, the abortive meeting between the conquerors and the Amerindian folk and, symbolically, the exploitation of land and people from time immemorial" (Maes-Jelinek 449).

Michael Anthony's *The Year in San Fernando* (1965), *The Games Were Coming* (1963), *Green Days by the River* (1967), and *Cricket in the Road* (1973) place the characters on a very simple setting of environmentalism. Edward Baugh explains about Anthony and his works:

> Concentrating on a careful recreation of the humble, ordinary life of the rural and semi-rural Trinidad of his youth, Anthony refreshes our awareness of the significance of the ordinary, and of how, in its simplest, homeliest motions, the heart can touch so much that is at once elemental and complex. His memory-sharpened evocations of particular place and time verify some basic, universal truths of the human condition. (81)

*The Year in San Fernando* forces us to see the landscape in a new way; a way that causes us to identify with it and appreciate it. Anthony brilliantly describes the cane fields, seasons, and rural and urban areas in a manner that depicts, foreshadows, and influences not only the social and political struggles of the characters, but also the growing consciousness of Francis, the protagonist. The watering of the plants for growth and the growth of the cane symbolize Francis' growth. The twelve-year old boy comes to urban San Fernando from rural Mayaro when the cane is young (chapter 6). While he experiences new things and grows, the cane becomes green (chapter 9). In chapter 18 the canefields are set on fire to burn or drive away unwanted elements like leaves and snakes in preparation for reaping, which signifies the passing of the boy's childhood. The cane is ready for harvest, in the next chapter, followed by the processing of the cane to sugar. Here, just after his mother's visit and departure, Francis—being processed by Julia, the boys at school, teachers, Mrs. Chandles' sickness, and family confusion—is prepared to accept fuller responsibilities. In chapter 26 the new stalks begin to grow as the rainy season begins symbolizing the beginning of a new stage or cycle—adolescence—of Francis' life.

Seasons and celebrations also have effect on the theme. Easter depicts the death, burial, resurrection, and ascension of Jesus Christ, but it also symbolizes the death of Francis' childhood and the resurrection of his adolescence. Christmas is the celebration of the birth of Christ, but in the novel it signifies the new birth of Francis, who is going home, at the end of the novel, as a new boy. The novel is set in the multiracial and multicultural Trinidad and Tobago, and written in a postcolonial era.[i] It asks the postcolonial question about the Caribbean's growth and progress; a question that other writers have asked. Samuel Selvon's *A Brighter Sun* (1952) has an Indian subject matter set in Trinidad and Tobago during World War II. At sixteen, Tiger is married to Urmilla through an arranged marriage, and he enters the adult world with its responsibilities and complexities. Tiger's closeness with nature parallels that of Francis'. American technological and materialistic pursuits of building a road at the naval base "changes the landscape and destroys the community's garden plots" (Fabre 112), but they also mature Tiger's consciousness and wisdom of embracing farming and his adult responsibilities.

In Caribbean literature, the concept of the strong mother figure features significantly, especially in relation with the land and the peoples' relationship with the land. The mother bears the responsibility of the family because the father is either dead or away from the home. In most cases an extra-marital relationship keeps him away from home, and in other cases he escapes into drunkenness. The result of this scenario promotes the mother as a heroine, for as a single parent she raises her family in a black working class setting. Many Caribbean novels are set in the working class tradition, and so the mother emerges as a figure of strength. But the strong mother figure also becomes a central postcolonial and multicultural metaphor of Caribbean life, culture, and literature. Jamaica Kincaid, Jean Rhys, Michelle Cliff, Maryse Conde, Paule Marshall, Zee Edgell, Christina Garcia, Erna Brodber, Lorna Goodison, Esmeralda Santiago, Wilson Harris, V. S. Naipaul, Samuel Selvon, Michael Anthony, Derek Walcott, George Lamming, Edward Kamau Brathwaite, and

Louise Bennett are some of the Caribbean writers who have given emphasis to the importance of the mother imagery in Caribbean literature in colonial, postcolonial, and multicultural settings. Reviewing Caroline Rody's *The Daughter's Return: African-American and Caribbean Women's Fictions of History*, Heather Hathaway illustrates Rody's argument that "due to the successive identification in the Caribbean of the mother-figure first with Europe during the colonial era, then with Africa during the rise of negritude, and finally with the islands themselves in contemporary post-colonial cultures, Caribbean writers portray "the mother" with considerable ambivalence" (2).

Jamaica Kincaid's depiction of the daughter's resistance to her mother's control and pursuit of freedom bears postcolonial and multicultural implications of the Caribbean's struggle for independence from the mother country and embracement of its mixed heritage, especially in *Annie John* (1985), *Lucy* (1990), *At the Bottom of the River* (1983), and *The Autobiography of My Mother* (1996). In Michelle Cliff's and Wilson Harris' works, the mother or daughter is identified with the land. Clare Savage in *No Telephone to Heaven* (1987) returns from America and England to the Caribbean to identify with the land and her people. Cliff points out:

> To write a complete Caribbean woman, or man for that matter, demands of us retracing the African past of ourselves, reclaiming as our own, and as our subject, a history sunk under the sea, or scattered as potash in the canefields, or gone to bush, or trapped in a class system notable for its rigidity and absolute dependence on color stratification. Or a past bleached from our minds. It means finding the artforms of those of our ancestors and speaking in the patois forbidden us. It means realizing our knowledge will always be wanting. It means also, I think, mixing in the forms taught us by the oppressor, undermining his language and co-opting his style, and turning it to our purpose. (*Abeng* 14)

In Rhys' *Wide Sargasso Sea* the biological mother disintegrates with the demise of the colonialism, but the Afro-Caribbean mother Christophine becomes Antoinette's strong surrogate mother. Antoinette's mother becomes insane. In fact she becomes so depressed by her first husband's death, the periods of separation from her second husband, and the chaotic slavery situations that she offers Antoinette very little help. However, Christophine, the black house servant, becomes Antoinette's mother and a figure of strength. In times of problems, she turns to Christophine for counsel, strength, and help. With Christophine by her side she grows stronger in confidence, but Rochester becomes threatened and insecure, so he sends the servant away. Without Christophine, Antoinette crumbles spiritually, socially, and psychologically. She cannot cope with her man-made problems. Jean Rhys' characterization of Christophine convinces us of the strength of the mother figure. Although the writer provides little physical description of her, she makes the servant's presence, power, and philosophy radiate throughout the novel. One hears the rhythm of her speech as powerful as one feels her presence as she advocates her feminist theory for Antoinette's survival: "Get up, girl, and dress yourself. Woman must have spunks to live in this wicked world" (101).

In *The Year in San Fernando*, Francis' father is dead and Ma labors as a domestic servant for a better future for her children. Ma seizes the opportunity for Francis to go to San Fernando to help the ailing, upper-class Mrs. Chandles. She sees this as a unique opportunity for her son to obtain a good education and escape from their life of rural poverty. When Ma visits Francis in San Fernando and prepares to leave, she earnestly encourages him to "Stay and take in education boy. Take it in. That's the main thing" (67). Similarly, Sophia Adams, in *Moon on a Rainbow Shawl*, also labors as a domestic servant to support her family, especially to help Esther to take the island scholarship. Although her husband, Charlie Adams, is not dead or separated from her, he becomes useless because his career in cricket has been strangled by the authorities, and he has no job. Charlie responds to his disillusionment by absenting himself from home most of the times and by getting drunk the rest of the times. "Set on a tropical island in the Caribbean [Trinidad and Tobago] in the late 1940s, *Moon* shows us how people deal with relationship problems, struggles against poverty and a willingness to better themselves, themes which are the same no matter what colour you are" (Orme). This multiracial, tenement yard community struggles against the tripartite colonial oppression of British colonialism, racial exploitation, and class discrimination.

In *Miguel Street* and *In the Castle of My Skin* the two boys, narrators, grow up without fathers. Both mothers strongly battle against the social and economic hardships to educate their sons for a better future. The mothers may severely punish their children out of frustration or from fear that the boys may stray from the right path of life, but they also know how important it is for the next generation to escape the aftermath of slavery and colonialism. All these mothers also recognize that education is the key to deliverance from the region's poverty. G's mother, in *In the Castle of My Skin*, bathes him naked while the other children climb on the fence and laugh. She lashes him to inculcate desirable behaviors, and even at eighteen when G prepares to leave the island for a job on another island, she spends hours lecturing to him about life. Similarly, the strong discipline of the narrator's mother in *Miguel Street* keeps him on the moral path of life and brings him success. Once she beats him so badly that he runs away to B. Wordsworth. He cries and decides not to return home, but with Wordsworth's help he returns a wiser boy. Likewise, Ti-Jean's mother, in *Ti-Jean and His Brothers*, becomes the voice of history, the connection between West Indians and nature and the environment, and the weapon of wisdom to defeat the devil/colonizer. These three mothers and other mothers in Caribbean literature become a postcolonial and multicultural voice forging a relationship between the land and the people. Lamming describes the voice of G's mother in a similar manner: "The mother of the novel is given no name. She is simply G's mother, a woman of little or no importance in her neighborhood until the tropical season rains a calamity on every household; and she emerges, without warning, as a voice of nature itself" (Introduction x).

The mother figure in Caribbean literature represents the symbol of origin, roots, and the land. In many cases, the writers illustrate the Caribbean man's relationship with the land by exploring the man's relationship with his mother. Since most of the writers write from a foreign land with a sense of nostalgia, they feel a special sense of responsibility to explore the complications of a West Indian's departure from his mother or land. At the end of *No Telephone to Heaven* Clare Savage has rejected her father's hypocritical obsession with his white color for her mother's wish: "I hope someday you make something of yourself, and someday help your people" (103). After a futile search for home in America and England, Clare returns to Jamaica, the land of her mother and grandmother's burial, where she is killed fighting for her people, but where her body becomes one with the land: "Clare's body is burned into the land by machine-gun fire, and as she loses consciousness, she slips from language into the preverbal, pre-literary sounds of a land before meaning, language, or symbolic use" (Raiskin 203). On another level, Christopher's identification with the land insists that he obtains a piece of land and bury his grandmother, although she has been dead "thirteen Chrismus" ago. He doesn't think it will hurt "the fat brown man in the big fat bed wrapped in flowers" (47) to give him a piece of land. But colonial greed from this suburban family refuses Christopher any land and results in their massacre.

Caribbean literature depicts the colonizer as the white male who exploits the land and the woman, and destroys or threatens to destroy the relationship between the woman and the landscape. The women, as mothers whose wombs produce fertility and life and wives whose love and romance anoint the bruised and battered bodies of colonized men, are in harmony with the landscape. And from this relationship they draw strength, healing, and inspiration. In Cliff's *No Telephone to Heaven*, Kitty's burial homage to her mother's body links her with her roots, identifies her with her homeland, and foreshadows her commitment to the land; a commitment that will cause her to deny America and her family for Jamaica, and one that will not allow her to leave for treatment in Miami:

When she dressed her mother's body, it was the first time she remembered seeing her mother's nakedness. The secret thing which had been hidden from her for thirty years became hers.... The breasts full—the nipples dark—were stiff with lifelessness, and she caressed them. From somewhere came an image of a slave-woman pacing aisles of cane, breasts slung over her shoulder to suckle the baby carried on her back. She kissed her mother on her eyelids and rubbed coconut oil across her body, into the creases and folds, softening the marks of childbearing and old age. (71-72)

Perhaps the strongest statement in favor of Caribbean environmental literature is depicted in Walcott's *Ti-Jean and His Brothers*, where the colonizer is also the planter, old man (Papa Bois), and the devil, whose nature and function are death and destruction: "The thief cometh not but to kill, and to steal, and to destroy" (John 10:10). The Bolom or foetus concords that the devil, his master, is responsible for evil, death, and destruction (99). He has no respect for the land, landscape, and the animals. Gros Jean and Mi-Jean are defeated and destroyed by the devil because they rely on their own strength—physical strength and book knowledge—respectively, and they disregard their mother's counsel to respect the environment (103, 104, 116). Gros Jean and Mi-Jean are victims of postcolonial deception and foolishness propagated through a colonial education, but Ti-Jean's common sense and respect for his mother, symbol of the land, elevate him to that status of David's triumph over Goliath. When he asks his mother for prayer, she remarks:

> The first of my children
> Never asked for my strength,
> The second of my children
> Thought little of my knowledge,
> The last of my sons, now,
> Kneels down at my feet,
> Instinct be your shield,
> It is wiser than reason,
> Conscience be your cause
> And plain sense be your sword.
> (Walcott, *Ti-Jean and His Brothers* 133-34)

Ti-Jean's success in defeating the devil is dependent on his mother's prayer for him and his obedience to his mother's counsel. Gros Jean's and Mi-Jean's failure to defeat the devil, however, is as a result of their pride and independence of their mother. She instructs Gros Jean in the ways of postcolonial and multicultural resistance:

> When you go down the tall forest, Gross Jean,
> Praise God who make all things; ask direction
> Of the bird, and the insects, imitate them;
> But becareful of the hidden nets of the devil,

> Beware of a wise man called Father of the Forest,
> The devil can hide in several features,
> A woman, a white gentleman, even a bishop.   (Walcott, *Ti-Jean and His Brothers* 103)

Ti-Jean believes his mother's prayer and counsel, heeds her words, and respects and compliments the creatures of the forest (135–37). His victory over the colonizer/planter/devil results from his harmonious relationship with his environment, the creatures of the forest, and his deep commitment to the land, mother. Gros Jean insults the animals: "Get out of my way, you slimy bastard! How God could make such things?" (104). Mi-Jean feels that Bird is disturbing him, and tells Bird: "Is animal you are, so please know your place" (115). His insults continue: "Frog,/You ever study your face in/The mirror of a pool?" (116).

This analytical and re-evaluative approach by Walcott and other Caribbean writers becomes a useful dialogue to stimulate the exploitation of history and imagination for progression and growth. As Caribbean writers, those mentioned and others like Martin Carter, Olive Senior, Louise Bennett, Jan Carew, Ismith Khan, and Edgar Mittleholzer evaluate and re-evaluate representations of the land and the peoples' relationships to their environments, they demonstrate intriguing shifts in perspectives, but they forge a new creation. Harris, in *The Whole Armour* and *A Palace of the Peacock*, depicts that history is a system of words not facts, and that the Caribbean is not the first land of slavery for the Africans, but that they were already slaves in Africa. Edward K. Brathwaite, in *The Arrivants*, a book of poetry, also explores this question of confrontation of the past. His re-evaluation of himself and his people influences the division of the book into three sections: "Rites of Passage" deals with the journey of Africans from Africa to the Caribbean as slaves, "Masks" takes us back to Africa to explore the culture and living conditions of the Africans, and "Islands" depicts slavery in the Caribbean. V. S. Naipaul uses a universal approach to evaluate and analyze himself and the Caribbean through his satire, sarcasm, irony, humor, and fictional autobiography. Along with the above, he employs caricature in presenting the "complex fate of the Caribbean," while Wilson Harris, John Hearne, George Lamming, Andrew Salkey, and Samuel Selvon pursue the rebuilding of the native's cultural image (Bhatnager 30–31), and each uses different techniques. Derek Walcott's re-evaluation focuses on the socio-political, economic, and cultural struggle which results from the Caribbean cultural pluralism. Walcott's artistic and dramatic approach incorporates his mulatto metaphor to depict the freshness and uniqueness of the Caribbean, while Lamming uses a Marxist approach to focus on the working class and their struggle to regain the land and save their environment from capitalistic corruption and exploitation. He believes that the working class will overthrow the oppressors. Michael Anthony forces his readers to look at the Caribbean from a different point of view, and then he asks about the future of postcolonial Caribbean. With such diversity of fictional and historical representations, nationhood and regionalism take shape. Indigenous Amerindians relate sacredly to the earth as their mother and God, Africans and Indians—emerging from slavery and indentureship, respectively—use the land and environment to fashion a new culture and belief, and at the same time their culture and belief shape the landscape, and Europeans exploit and destroy the land and environment. History informs, vision and imagination create, and "with this prodigious ambition one began" ("What the Twilight Says" 4).

# Note

1. Trinidad and Tobago gained its independence on August 31, 1962.

# CHAPTER FIVE

# Colonialism and Capitalism: Biblical Allusion of the Corrupting Force of Money in Selected Caribbean Literature

According to Randy Alcorn, money has two faces. It is used to feed, clothe, house, build churches, spread the gospel, alleviate suffering, and provide betterment for people. Money is a tool to facilitate and expedite trade. It allows flexibility and convenience. God encouraged the people of Israel to make use of the convenience of money. Because of distance, he told them to exchange the tithes (crops and livestock) for silver (money), then convert it back to the goods of their choice once they arrived at the place of worship (Duet. 14:24-26). But it is also used to buy a slave, swindle a widow's land, purchase sexual favors, bribe a judge, and peddle drugs (33-37). Paul warns about the other side of money: "People who want to get rich fall into temptation and a trap and into many foolish and harmful desires that plunge men into ruin and destruction. For the love of money is a root of all kinds of evil" (1 Tim. 6:9-10). Numerous biblical incidents and characters warn against the danger of loving money. Achan's lust for materialism brought death to himself, family, and other men in battle (Josh. 7), the Prophet Balaam would have cursed God's people for payment from Balak (Num. 22:4-35), Delilah betrayed Samson to the Philistines for a fee (Judg. 16), Solomon's lust for more wealth led him to disobey the prohibitions of God's law concerning the accumulation of large amount of gold, silver, horses, and wives (Duet.

17:16-17), Gehazi lied to Naaman and then to Elisha, in order to gain wealth, for which he was punished with leprosy (2 Kings 5 20-27), Ananias and Sapphira withheld money they said was given to the Lord and were struck dead for it (Acts 5:1-11), the materialist Judas asked the chief priests, "What are you willing to give me if I hand him over to you?" then betrayed the Son of God for thirty pieces of silver (Matt. 26:14-16, 47-50; 27:3-10). Jesus warned against any form of excessive love for money: "Watch out! Be on your guard against all kinds of greed; a man's life does not consist in the abundance of his possessions" (Luke 12:15).

For Karl Marx, in a colonial society, capitalism, exploitation, and alienation are interwoven in their web-like destructive force. Marx took an economic approach to alienation, concerning "himself with the workers of the world: labor and its economic powerlessness" (Joseph 7). Alienation from self, for Marx, means,

> 'estrangement from the things,' which means the alienation of the worker from the product of his labor—that is, the alienation of that which mediates his relation to the 'sensual external world' and hence to the objects of nature. What the worker produces is not his own, but rather someone else's; it meets not his own needs; it is a commodity he sells to eke out a bare existence. The more he produces, the more his product and hence the objects of nature stand opposed to him. (Bulhan 186)

> Marx's influence can be traced in Fanon's concurrence that alienation is primarily economic: "If there is an inferiority complex, it is the outcome of a double process:— primarily, economic;—subsequently, the internalization—or, better, the epidermalization—of this inferiority" (Fanon, Introduction to *Black Skin*, 11).

Economics, according to Rodney and Memmi, is at the center of colonization[1]. It is also the core of Antoinette Cosway/Mason/Rochester's tragedy. Margaret Paul Joseph's study of the importance of mirror as a reflection of otherness alludes to economic exploitation. Joseph argues that "the basis of the whole story is again a matter of economics...but wealth is turned into a major symbol of evil. Money is a corrupting influence and is linked to betrayal, revenge, and power." Continuing to illustrate how the power of money becomes the greatest evil, since money can ruin people's lives, Joseph advocates that "Annette Mason and Antoinette Cosway are both victims of Englishmen who, like countless others before them, went to the colonies to make money with no regard for the consequences on the lives of the people who lived there" (33-34). This chapter demonstrates the role the love of money plays in Antoinette's tragedy.

Gossiping ex-slaves perceptively point out that Mr. Mason "didn't come to the West Indies to dance—he came to make money as they all do. Some of the big estates are going cheap, and one unfortunate's loss is always a clever man's gain" (29–30)[2]. As one of Antoinette's colonizer/Prospero, Mr. Mason's marriage to Annette sparks hostility from the ex-slaves. The marriage also leads to Antoinette's tragedy and alienation. Joseph explains that "the rich Mr. Mason (so sure of himself, so English in his confidence, thinks Antoinette) marries Mrs. Cosway and saves the estate they all love; but in true Prospero fashion he is insensitive to the mood of the laborers on the island and this brings tragedy to his wife and her children" (34). Failing to discern the ex-slaves' changing attitude, Mason assures Annette: "You were the widow of a slave-owner, the daughter of a slave-owner, and you had been living here alone, with two children, for nearly five years," but Annette perceptively points out her new economic status' influence on the ex-slaves: "We were so poor then...we were something to laugh at. But we are not poor now.... You are not a poor man. Do you suppose that they don't know all about your estate in Trinidad? And the Antigua property?" (32). Later, Antoinette interprets economics as the basis of her alienation: "The black people did not hate us quite so much when we were poor. We were white but we had not escaped and soon we would be dead for we had no money left. What was there to hate?" (34). Howells summarizes that Annette's "alliance with the new colonialism" sparks new implications (110), and Emery concurs that "Annette's marriage solidifies the power of the neocolonialists; it also intensifies the conflict between blacks and whites. The blacks call them "white Cockroach," but the whites call them "white niggers" (102, 100). Whites alienate Annette's family on the basis of her low economic status, while blacks alienate them on the basis of her high economic status. Howells sums up this tragedy: "Hated by the blacks and despised for their poverty by both blacks and other whites, Antoinette and her mother are the victims of a system the collapse of which has not only dispossessed them as a class but also deprived them as individuals of any means of independent survival" (110).

Steeped in typical colonizer's overconfidence and arrogance, Mason's late-rescue-attempt is futile. Coulibri has been set on fire, Pierre, Antoinette's little retarded brother, is killed, Antoinette is hurt, and Annette goes mad. "Indirectly, Mason is the cause of her madness," claims Joseph, but he also causes Antoinette's displacement and alienation (35). Robbed of her mother, brother, stepfather, Tia, Christophine, and Coulibri, Antoinette is placeless. After her recuperation at Aunt Cora's house, Antoinette is placed in a convent, "a place of...death" (56), where she prays "for a long time to be dead" (57).

Unaware of and unconcerned about his role in Annette's tragedy, Mason, "grinning hypocrite" and "coward" (40, 47), blindly lays the foundation for

Antoinette's tragedy by means of an arranged marriage. He supplies the dowery and arranges the marriage: "I want you to be happy, Antoinette, secure, I've tried to arrange.... I have asked some English friends to spend next winter here. You won't be dull" (59). Ironically, just the announcement of this colonial/patriarchal news produces "a feeling of dismay, sadness," and "loss," leading to the second dream which expands the first and foreshadows the colonial and patriarchal oppression and exploitation. The first dream occurs at Coulibri (26-27), and it is repeated two times (59-60, 187-90), each time with "more clarity and detail" (Olaussen 70). It also suggests Antoinette's "fear of sexual violation" (70). The second dream, like the first, precedes Antoinette's tragedy. It prophesies her marriage and so-called madness, links with Mason's manipulating role in marriages, and leaves Antoinette in loneliness. It also foreshadows "Antoinette's departure from the primeval forest of the West Indies to the imprisoning, enclosed garden that is England" (Friedman 125).

Where Mr. Mason's colonizing/patriarchal work ends, his son from a previous marriage and Antoinette's stepbrother, Richard Mason, commences. Richard is at the center of Antoinette's arranged marriage. He panics at Antoinette's reluctance to go through with the marriage (78-79) and gives Antoinette strong "arguments, threats probably," forcing her to keep the arrangement (90-91). Rochester distrusts him (91), and Christophine "is right to blame Richard Mason for his stepsister's affairs" (Le Gallez 143). Christophine echoes Richard's dark side: "Law! The Mason boy fix it, that boy worse than Satan and he burn in hell one of these fine nights" (110). Aunt Cora's argument with Richard Mason also illuminates his corruption: "You are handing over everything the child owns to a perfect stranger" (114).

From Mr. Mason to Richard Mason to Edward Rochester, their economic exploitation of Antoinette fosters her alienation. Rochester's, Antoinette's greatest colonizer, "moral decline of a 'gentle, generous' and 'brave' soul...may be traced to his materialism" (Le Gallez 141). Fragmented and exploited by his wealthy father willing all the family money to the older brother, "Edward is expected to contribute further to that status by taking part in an arranged marriage with a wealthy heiress" in order not to weaken the family status (141). Thus, his hypocritical playacting before the marriage is "a faultless performance," filled with "effort of will," rather than love, leaves Antoinette's hand "cold as ice in the hot sun," and deludes all except the blacks (76-77).

In typical colonial-imposing fashion, Rochester sweeps over Antoinette's fear, concern, and reluctance in preference for his "sad heart," the arrangement, and the "role of rejected suitor jilted by this creole girl" (78-79), because of the strong economic motivation and dictation. The colonizer/Rochester's main objective in a/the relationship with the colony/Antoinette is to 'rape' her and extract all her wealth. Rochester admits his quest for exploitation: "I didn't love her. I was thirsty for her, but that is not love. I felt very little tenderness for her, she was a stranger to me, a stranger who did not think or feel as I did" (93). And "the lack of any 'married woman's property act' ensures that Antoinette's money, on her marriage to Edward, becomes absorbed into his own estate" (Le Gellez 142). Even in the penultimate paragraph of Rochester's narration, as he prepares to return to England, he is obsessed with Antoinette's money: "I'd sell the place for what it would fetch. I had meant to give it back to her. Now—what's the use?" (173). But his letters to his greedy, exploitative father have already provided insights into this economic transaction which leaves Antoinette "a displaced person in her own country" (Howells 111). The letters authenticate that "thirty thousand pounds have been paid to me [Rochester] without question or condition," and that "no provision" has been "made for her" [Antoinette] (70).

Antoinette's money, now in the greedy, grasping hands of Rochester, drives the swindler Daniel Cosway to blackmail for a share of it. Cosway's revengeful exploitation climaxes Rochester's final stranglehold on Antoinette. Daniel Cosway's Eurocentric, epistolary method of communication to Rochester parallels Rochester's letters to his father, since both emerge out of a deep fragmented psyche and both seek to extract different measures of recompense. Furthermore, "Rochester, like Cosway, turns hate for his father into hate for Antoinette," claims Angier. She further compares: "Cosway and Rochester share similar characters—even to their ultimate greed, which each gives rein to through a self-righteous desire for vengeance" (162). Cosway's first letter to Rochester alludes to money several times and to the revenge motif: "My momma die when I was quite small and my godmother take care of me. The old mister [Antoinette's father] hand out some money for that though he don't like me. No, that old devil don't like me at all, and when I grow older I see it and I think, Let him wait my day will come" (96). But Antoinette's father and mother are deceased, thereby aborting his plans for revenge. However, Antoinette remains his target, and he, like his namesake, Esau, believes that "vengeance is mine" (122). Cosway also knows that Mr. Mason has given Antoinette half of his money when he died (97). Cosway wants some of that money, so he mixes facts and fiction to extract money from Rochester, and in the process he further destroys Antoinette's life, love, and marriage. His second letter not only reveals his wickedness, but also his coerciveness: "You want me to come to your house and bawl out your business before everybody? You come to me or I come" (119). Moreover, Amélie confirms Daniel Cosway's imitation of white people and his mysterious life (120-21), while Cosway himself displays his blackmail: "'But if I keep my mouth shut it seems to me you

owe me something. What is five hundred pounds to you. To me it's my life....
And if I don't have the money I want you will see what I can do'" (126).

Immediately after reading Cosway's letter, Rochester crushes the flower,
foreshadowing his crushing of Antoinette's spirit. He sweats, trembles, sees the
day as "far too hot" (99), looks like he has seen a zombie (100), gets lost and
becomes afraid (105), and tightens his grip of alienation on Antoinette. He
has bound her into economic dependence, rendering her unable to initiate or
execute escape. Antoinette explains her economic bondage: "He would never
give me any money to go away and he would be furious if I asked him. There
would be a scandal if I left him and he hates scandal. Even if I got away (and
how?) he would force me back. So would Richard. So would everybody else.
Running away from him, from this island, is the lie" (113). (A version of this
section re-appears in chapter seven in a wider discussion on alienation in *Wide
Sargasso Sea*).

Antoinette, like Jesus, has been betrayed. Judas, the treasurer, loved
money so much that he sold his master for thirty pieces of silver. In Antoinette's case there is much buying, selling, and betrayal. Rochester has sold his
soul for thirty thousand pounds (70), but in so doing he has aided and abetted
the selling of Antoinette's body, soul, and spirit for minus thirty thousand
pounds and property. Such grave devaluation and dehumanization of Antoinette results from the colonizers' (Mason, Richard, Rochester, and his father)
love for money. Christophine perceptively informs Antoinette about Rochester's love for money: "'Your husband certainly love money.... That is no lie.
Money have pretty face for everybody, but for that man money pretty like
pretty self, he can't see nothing else'" (114). Indeed, Rochester's excessive and
compulsive love for money, a colonialistic feature, blinds his moral and spiritual eyes.

Rochester cannot see Antoinette's beauty and tragedy, the landscape's
beauty, nor his action's corruption. For the wounded and fragmented Rochester, "everything is too much.... Too much blue, too much purple, too much
green. The flowers are too red, the mountains are too high, the hills too near.
And the woman is a stranger" (70). Coming from a cold and corrupted culture, Rochester fails to love Antoinette and cannot understand and appreciate
her love. Staley enlightens that "Edward comes from another world and cannot fathom the life of the passions; everything in the natural surroundings
which epitomizes sensuous beauty tells him that this is Antoinette's world, and
this is why he fears it from the beginning" (114–15). He wants an object and a
passive partner, but his failure to control and dominate the landscape renders
him powerless: "I wanted to say something reassuring but the scent of the river
flowers was overpoweringly strong. I felt giddy" (83), and it also symbolizes his

inability to celebrate the colorful and passionate personality and sexuality of his wife. Threatened and terrified by the landscape, a fearful Rochester "broke a spray off and trampled it into the mud" (99), and his cold and callous way of destroying the landscape symbolizes the way he destroys Antoinette in order to control her. His greedy thirst/lust cannot be satisfied because his colonial perspective associates his hatred to Antoinette and her landscape:

> I hated the mountains and the hills, the rivers and the rain. I hated the sunsets of whatever color, I hated its beauty and its magic and the secret I would never know. I hated its indifference and the cruelty which was part of its loveliness. Above all I hated her. For she belonged to the magic and the loveliness. She had left me thirsty and all my life would be thirst and longing for what I had lost before I found it. (172)

This heavenly place where Antoinette belongs and where she wishes to stay (108), has been made into a hell by Rochester: "But I loved this place and you have made it into a place I hate. I used to think that if everything else went out of my life I would still have this, and now you have spoilt it. It's just somewhere else where I have been unhappy, and the other things are nothing to what has happened here" (147).

Rochester makes love to the rebellious, Amélie, next to his wife's room, and forms another economic exploitative union: "'But she love money like you love money—must be why you come together. Like goes to like'" (149), insinuates Christophine. And Antoinette rebukes Rochester's hypocrisy by comparing him to slave masters: "'You abused the planters and made up stories about them, but you do the same thing. You send the girl away quicker, and with no money or less money, and that's all the difference'" (146). And his monetary present ushers the girl into a life of prostitution to satisfy her love for money (140–41). Additionally, Rochester is willing to pay double and even triple to alienate Antoinette in his frigid attic and to maintain absolute silence (177–78). And Mrs. Eff and Grace Poole serve the devil for money because service to Rochester parallels service to the devil (177). Thus, by the end of the novel, the colonized, Antoinette, remains free from the clutches of the love of money, but the colonizer, Rochester, becomes possessed with money. His cold, callous heart would not allow him to leave Antoinette in the Caribbean, nor would it allow him to give her any of her own money. Rather, one form of corruption breeds another, and the more money he gets, the more dissatisfied he is. Despite his profession of religion (127), he has forgotten biblical warnings, stated earlier. He is also too blind to see truth in the testimonies of some of the world's wealthiest men. John D. Rockefeller postulates: "I have made many millions, but they have brought me no happiness," W. H. Vanderbilt agrees that "the care of $200,000,000 is enough to kill anyone.

There is no pleasure in it," John Jacob Astor confesses: "I am the most miserable man on earth," and Andrew Carnegie acknowledges that "millions seldom smile" (qtd. in Alcorn 69). Furthermore, secular religion fails to adhere to Christ's warning against laying up treasures on earth, and worrying about material things (Matt. 6:25–34), and refuses to learn from Solomon's observation that "the sleep of the laborer is sweet, whether he eats little or much, but the abundance of a rich man permits him no sleep" (Eccles. 5:12).

Rochester has now inherited all Antoinette's money and "everything" from his family (177), yet he spends extravagantly on the marginalization of Antoinette, but not on her therapy, or freedom.

## Color Complication and Confrontation in Caribbean Culture as Depicted in Trevor Rhone's *Old Story Time*

Scholarship is meaningless, pointless, and futile when the academy is isolated and alienated from the community, when it does not teach, effect, and change society, and when it does not learn from the community. Scholars whose works reflect little or no relationship with the community are like porcupines that attend a porcupine dance. They come and go without any involvement or connection. John Donne's statement, "No man is an Iland, intire of it selfe;/... any man's death diminishes me,/because I am involved in Mankinde" serves to enlighten present-day scholarship for tomorrow's realization of desirability and wholeness. Against this background, I hasten to ponder aloud a few thought processes. Are people of European heritage really white, and people of African heritage really black? Where does the rest of the world fit in this color dichotomy? How did humanity get caught-up in this hostile black and white contradiction? Will there ever be an era that is free from color consciousness and color discrimination? Fanon believes that "the fact of the juxtaposition of the white and black races has created a massive psycho existential complex" (*Black Skin* 12). He further believes that analysis through scholarship can help to destroy this complex (12).

My wife is of African heritage and I am of Asian, Indian heritage. During the hundred plus years of slavery and the hundred plus years of colonization—particularly indentureship—in the Caribbean, much hybridization, mongrelization, bastardization, and schizophrenization have taken place. Apart from the difficulty of deciphering the pain of the past and forging the focus of the future, the result of such processes can be catastrophic on the basis of color complication. In my family and my wife's family lineages there are relatives who are extremely dark and those who are extremely fair in complexion. Our children have different shades of pigmentation, and at times I find myself try-ing to figure out the nature of each child's future confrontation with color prejudices and discriminations. Additionally, the memory of my mother's at-tachment of the adjective "black" to any negative statement given to my sister of dark complexion and the haunting effects of those verbal insults on my sis-ter's life continue to create hallucinations of color complication in my mind for my children's lives. Her use of the word *black* suggests not only color, but also race and ethnicity. Her repeated warnings that I can marry any girl except a "black" girl meant not so much that I should abstain from marrying a girl of dark complexion—though that was an important consideration—but that I was debarred from marrying someone from African heritage. Set against the racial war and killing in the formerly British Guiana in the early 1960s—the eve of independence—how could I become involved with humanity when I could not cross, emotionally, the boundaries of our yard since my two next door neigh-bors happened to be black in color and race, though I crossed physically? My narrowly confined world afforded little or no opportunity for conscious or un-conscious decolonization. Societal and parental marginalization was well de-fined and defended. Therefore, my first two romantic relationships had to be terminated the moment they unsettled the society, the status-quo, and our parents, because they were interracial. The society, a victim of the past, squeezed our parents into its mould, and forced them to act as robots to its racial, stereotypical dictates. Pondering and reflecting on the past lead me to question the future. Will the twenty-first century eradicate and transcend the social and political barriers of color? Based on the track record of the past centuries, there is little hope, but there is more hope on the basis of spiritual revival and academic scholarship. This section explores the creation and con-sumption of color discrimination through colonization and the complex fate of the Caribbean in a color conscious community as depicted in Trevor Rhone's *Old Story Time*.

Color, a major tool of colonization, becomes associated with race, class, and gender in its mission of oppression and exploitation. Before Christopher Columbus' rediscovery of the West Indies in 1492, native West Indians or Amerindians were color blind, but Europeans came, saw, and conquered. They dictated the organization of class and power structure on the basis of color; white was might. They then complicated the structure with the intro-duction of Africans as slaves. With the genocide of Amerindians, except in Dominica and Guyana, where they have been driven deeper into the jungle, the power structure was white and black, European and African, master and slave, and Prospero and Caliban. After theoretical abolition of slavery in 1834, however, several attempts to replace plantation labor force failed until Indians were lured to and kept in the Caribbean, under fraudulent and slavish contracts. Through the famous colonial system of divide and rule, whites now complicated the color and the power structure by deflating black hostility to brown passivity. African West Indians felt cheated with the intrusion of other races, and they responded to the presence of these other races, particularly Indians (people from India) because of their own fear and insecurity—manipulated by the colonizers. By this time mulattoes—bastards, mongrels, schizophrenics,[3] and hybrids—emerged in a multitude of color variation. These were the children of mixed relationships—especially black and white and black and brown.

In *Black Skin*, Fanon documents that gulfs existed among these groups. Prospero, Caliban, and Ariel have created through cross-fertilization intriguingly beautiful bastards. But the colonizers have never changed the power structure to accommodate these variations. Thus, displacement, discrimination, and degradation have erupted in this vicious colonial cycle of color marginalization. West Indians, therefore, have the Herculean task of resistance and decolonization, especially in the area of color. Their method and success of decolonization, though, would depend largely on their geographical, political, and socio-economic locations; and these factors raise intricate faculties for research and scholarship. Trevor Rhone's *Old Story Time* illustrates the effects of colonization's use of color in the Caribbean, Sam Selvon's *The Lonely Londoners* demonstrates the destructive forces of color against West Indians in England, and Michelle Cliff's *No Telephone to Heaven* postulates that color, as a colonial agent, is very much alive in the United States of America. Color, therefore, follows West Indians throughout the world—fragmenting and displacing them—as well as complicating their search for identity.

Trevor Rhone's *Old Story Time's* exploration of attitudes to color reveals the problematizations of a color-complicated culture created through colonization in the Caribbean. According to Mervyn Morris, "the play travels the journey of Jamaican society in the last three or four decades, from a time when colour discrimination was the norm and was accepted by its victims, into an era when a few blacks slipped through the net into further education; and unto the period when those educated blacks, in the new political climate, begin to be appointed to positions of power" (X). Against this colonial backdrop, on the eve of independence, the characters are caught in a delicate and complicated frame of time and action. They are controlled by the past, and yet their future depend largely on their ability to break out of the cage of present social, economic, and spiritual bondage which creates family and relationship conflicts. Miss Aggy's color purgatory springs from her brainwash by a lopsided colonial education, which has taught her that black is degration and degeneration, while white is advancement and creative. She beats Len, her son, out of a childhood relationship with Pearl, the barefoot girl, and indoctrinates him that Margaret, Reverend Greaves' brownskin daughter, is advancement:

Miss Esmeralda frowsy-tail, jiggerfoot, jeysey ears, board head gal is your friend? Where is yuh ambition? Yuh don't have any ambition? After A struggle out mi soul case to send you to big shot high school, you come home come mix up with that little dry-head gal? How much time A must tell you, anything black nuh good? She is no advancement. It look like A will have to beat it in you. [*She drags him up.*] A will hang you, you know. Them little dry-head gal will drag you down! [*As she pushes him to the ground again.*] You think A want to treat you like this? A only want what is best for you ...Leave out the dutty black gal them, concentrate on yuh books, for life is hard when you black, but with a little education you still have a chance. When time come for you to have girlfriend, A have a nice girl picked out for you. Miss Margaret, Reverend Greaves daughter, a nice brown girl with tall hair down to her back. She is advancement, you hear me. [*She picks him up*]. (14)

Miss Aggy's self-contracdiction is reflective of postcolonial Caribbean's internal conflict, which has been afflicted by the mother country, Britain. Her insight leads to an awareness of the connection between class and color and education and freedom, but her blindness desensitizes her of the new form of enslavement and castration she causes Len. The son must fulfill the mother's unrealized dreams of escaping, at any cost, her lower class status through education and marriage, which have enormous hurdles of color to leap over. In leaping over these hurdles, however, Len drifts away from Miss Aggy, the new agent of color colonization, but closer to Miss Aggy's reflection, Miss Lois. Len's teenage experiences of humiliation, public abuse, and psychological castration have been hidden from Miss Aggy, but communicated to Lois. In utter ignorance that Blackie is now Dr. Tomlinson, or Len, George ironically recounts Len's public humiliation on Open Day when the boy's mother slips, falls, and spills the contents of her basket. Spilling the contents of the basket—bananas, yams, cocoas, etc.—becomes a betrayal of the secrecy of poverty, whose marriage with race and color creates triple marginalization.

Miss Aggy pressures Len into the trap of color castration. Using Len's love letter to Margaret as bait, George and his gang lure Len into a physical beating and psychological castration. As Len screams in pain and runs away, George announces, "that'll teach you, lover boy! That'll teach you. Next time we cut it off. This was just a rehearsal. Next time it's for real" (84). These episodes demonstrate the enormity of the damage done to Len's psyche and identity. Throughout Len's school life, he cannot match the other boys because the scale of power and authority is controlled by color. Len's color places him at the bottom of the scale, and his mother's racial and socio-economic positions add to the liability of his self-esteem. She is a black, poor, single parent, who is totally unaware of the tragedy her obsession with color has caused her son. Len becomes the "invisible man," "the mascot," and "the laughing stock" of the class.

Paradoxically, though, Miss Aggy may have demonstrated gross ignorance and callousness in her degrading description of Pearl, but later she justifies her behavior as necessary precaution for Len's protection. Pearl's degenerated condition—pregnant with her sixth child and showing marks of harassment by careless men—serves as justification for Miss Aggy's strong hand in Len's upbringing: "When me look on her, an' think say if me never did fight an' struggle with the one Mass Len, all now him would be knocking 'bout the district a turn wutliss like the rest a them" (17-18). Later, Miss Aggy begins to demonstrate signs of compassion. Touched by Pearl's further depravation and poverty—pregnant with her twelfth child, she intercedes for Len to help Pearl financially. Indeed another paradox arises from Miss Aggy's rejection of Pearl and Lois because of their color. For her abhorrence of "anything black" leads her into devilish obsession and possession to the point of murdering any black chicken in her yard (14). She further complicates colonial cultural and educational imposition through self-denial and resistance to change. With her own lot she is content, but paradoxically, she covets something better for her son: "Black was good enough for me. It not good enough for him. There was better for him" (23). Like her predecessors, Miss Aggy practices the theory of emancipation from colonial oppression and marginalization on the bases of race and color—sacrifice of the present generation for the freedom of the future generation.

Rhone is careful here to redirect our hostility away from Miss Aggy to the colonial system through its use of a color chart marginalization. In my interview with Rhone, in March, 1998, he pointed out that after the emancipation of slavery in the Caribbean, his ancestry moved as far as possible away from the plantation, a place of oppression, exploitation, and marginalization. In Bellas Gate, a village in St. Catherine where he grew up, there was no racial and color barrier. The rurality of Bellas Gate and his strict, religious parents reinforced color blindness in the young dramatist's mind, but then in secondary school at Bedford and Smith's (now St. Jago High School) in Spanish Town, he was shocked at the color conflicts between Blacks and Whites, Jews and Gentiles. At high school Rhone became aware of a color discrimination chart by the teacher, where students were treated and respected on the basis of their color. In awarding 12 "Boy of the Week Awards" to 26 boys, the teacher started with the whitest boys, moving from white to brown to black. Students recognized the creation of a graded color chart from which they could predict the names of number six, seven, and eight, but they also knew that there were not enough weeks in the semester to reach them if they were black in complexion. The Calibans of the class were forced to react to the color scheme of marginalization. Rhone and his friend used razorblades to mutilate the awards canvas board. The color chart board was never restored. That was Rhone's first response to racial and color discrimination.

Rhone's decolonization of the old colonial myth that Caliban is the "dark thing," the evil, becomes an authentic and dramatic contribution of postcolonial writers' task of setting the records straight and telling the whole story in context. The burden of proof rests on these writers whose task is not only to objectively refute the erroneous distortions of colonization in the name of history, but also to re-create the truth of color discrimination. George McFarlane, the representation of the colonizer through color as well as the Arielic collaborator with Prospero, is the devil that has come to kill and to steal and to destroy (Jn. 10:10). George spins a web of economic and moral fraud and corruption. This mulatto villain swindles money from different ones, including Miss Aggy, blackmails Lois into moral and financial compromise, and threatens to blackmail Len. Caught in a time of change, George becomes Judas. He holds on to the past— which represents his security at the expense of the poverty and suffering of blacks, preoccupies himself with fraudulent money transactions, and becomes unpatriotic to the new Jamaica. Morris concludes that George is "ubiquitously evil: assisted by Margaret, he has been cruel to Len at school; he is responsible for a painful episode in Lois's past; ...George is a sinner whom the play does not redeem" (xi). His lack of redemption, however, is contrasted with Miss Aggy's painful and difficult deliverance, decolonization, and redemption.

Profound subservience to fairer skins leads to Miss Aggy's slow recognition of George's crookedness (Morris xi). Initially, she sees him as her God-sent angel: "Is God send you here to guide and look after me, you know. Lord, yes, a house for mi son. Lord, yes! Thank you, Missa Mac, thank you" (36). But the devil is transformed into the light of an angel (2 Cor. 11:14), tricking us into believing that he is the god of this world through the blinding of minds (2 Cor. 4: 4). Miss Aggy sees Len's refusal to help George out of his financial corruption and dilemma as evil and ungrateful: "Is a good opportunity to repay the debt we owe the family. His father-in-law feed you when I was down and out. I remember and I am grateful" (58). The scales of color marginalization and colonial domination are too heavy on Miss Aggy's eyes. They prevent her from discerning the irony of George's evil: "No! Black people too wicked and bad. Missa Mac say you could help him. If not for him, then for Miss Margaret. Is God send you this opportunity. Help them for Mama's sake" (59).

Miss Aggy's "animosity is directed against her own colour; against Lois, the black girl who, she fears, must have captured Len by obeah; against the woman who, in the end, will so generously forgive" (Morris xi). Her confrontation with Lois—a reminder and reflection of her own color—is a confrontation of her denied self, which colonization has taught her to despise and deny. But Christ-like love, patience, and compassion, demonstrated, not by the religious and pharisaic Reverend Greaves and his daughter, but by Lois, her father, and Pa Ben, facilitate Miss Aggy's rescue from colonial color slavery and Len's from the postcolonial trap of revenge. Lois and her father are the good Samaritans who have ministered to Len's wounds on the night of his beating, and who have supported Len—especially financially—to complete his doctorate in England (85). In like manner, Pa Ben places less emphasis on color in his scale of values. Love matters most to him, and he seeks to transcend the earthly for the heavenly: "He deplores Miss Aggy's hostile reaction to her son having married black. When there is a quarrel, Pa Ben is ready to forgive; and he is patient enough to wait until Miss Aggy, after more than a year, begins to acknowledge him again. He tackles obstacles to love ...Through times of adversity, Pa Ben remains the faithful friend, the instrument of peace, the soul of love" (Morris xi).

The point Rhone underscores here is the point many other Caribbean writers have made and are making, and that is the role of the ordinary people of the Caribbean in decolonization. Derek Walcott's *Ti-Jean and His Brothers* reinforces the conviction that the little people or the ordinary people's use of common sense is a strong tool of resistance. Ti-Jean (Little John, the man of color, with practicality and common sense), not Gros-Jean (Big John full of physical strength, but little intellectual power) and Mi-Jean (Middle John, who has too much intellectual power, but little common sense), is the force of resistance that is capable of defeating the colonial oppressive powers of the Old Man/Papa Bois/Planter. In Jean Rhys' *Wide Sargasso Sea*, the black Christophine serves as the tower of strength for Antoinette, but she has become the major force of opposition to Rochester's colonial and patriarchal enslavement.

In the old colonial exploitation and oppression on the basis of color, has blacks' demonstration of resilience and love to forgive the oppressors ever been historically and publicly registered? Martin Luther King, Jr. and Mahatma Gandhi's non-violence resistance to colonial and racial marginalization and oppression, along with Bishop Desmond Tutu and the South African Amnesty Commission, are but a few contemporary redemptive agents. These legacies remind us that in every sphere of human life and activity, there is a great need for ambassadors of reconciliation (2 Cor. 5:16–21), who will teach and demonstrate that "racial [color] reconciliation is built on the foundation of committed relationships" (Ruth 1:1, Kehrein and Washington 113), and it takes "purposeful, positive, and planned activity" (Eph. 2:14–15, Kehrein and Washington 125) to further enhance King's dream of a day when by faith "we will be able to transform the jangling discords of our nation into a symphony of harmony" ("I Have a Dream"). But for the Caribbean, this dream is still illusive.

# Notes

1. Memmi's statement reinforces the point that "colonization is, above all, economic and political exploitation" (149).

2. The ex-slaves also allude that Mr. Cosway's, Antoinette's father, degenerated economy, resulting from emancipation, has caused his death (28).

3. My use of the word schizophrenics is not in the medical sense, but cultural, racial, and biological mixtures.

# CHAPTER SIX

# Disorder and Mimicry through Colonial Apparatuses in V. S. Naipaul's *The Mimic Men*

The outer and inner worlds do not have the physical separateness which they had for us in Trinidad. They coexist; the society only pretends to be colonial; and for this reason its absurdities are at once apparent. Its mimicry is both less and more than a colonial mimicry. It is the special mimicry of an old country which has been without a native aristocracy for a thousand years and has learned to make room for outsiders, but only at the top. The mimicry changes, the inner world remains constant: this is the secret of survival. And so it happens that, to one whole area of India, a late seventeenth century traveler like Ovington remains in many ways a reliable guide. Yesterday the mimicry was Mongul; tomorrow it might be Russian or American; today it is English.

Mimicry might be too harsh a word for what appears so comprehensive and profound: buildings, railways, a system of administration, the intellectual discipline of the civil servant and the economist. Schizophrenia might better explain the scientist who, before taking up his appointment, consults the astrologer for an auspicious day. But mimicry must be used because so much has been acquired that the schizophrenia is often concealed; because so much of what is seen remains simple mimicry, incongruous and absurd; and because no people, by their varied physical endowments are as capable of mimicry as the Indians. (Naipaul, *An Area of Darkness* 56-57)

On the evening of the twentieth century—which has seen the partial destruction of oppressive systems like colonialism and apartheid—and the morning of the twenty-first century—which has violently shocked our world into fear and insecurity—many marginalized peoples seek drastic ways to confront the past and create and reach for a brighter horizon.[1] The past of slavery, colonization, apartheid, war, oppression, and discrimination is vividly depicted through the bizarre lives of Bigger Thomas, Frederick Douglass, Harriet Jacobs, Sula, Celie, Obi, Okonkwo, Bakha, Moraes Zogoiby called "Moor," Esthappen and Rahel, Willieboy, Antoinette, Boesman, and Lena. But V. S. Naipaul's mimic man, Ralph Singh, remains the most dramatic portrayal of the shattering and shipwrecking effects of colonization. Although much of the body of criticism on *The Mimic Men* focus on narrative technique, writing, the artist, autobiography, personal and political corruption, no in-depth study has analyzed Ralph Singh's tragedy as a direct effect of colonization. From a postcolonial and multicultural perspective, this chapter demonstrates how several colonial apparatuses act as agents of disorder and mimicry in Ralph Singh's life.[2]

While colonialism has created Karl Marx by capitalistic exploitation, Garibaldi by Sicilian poverty, Lenin by Russian autocracy, Gandhi by British imperialism, and Fanon by white racism (Caute 2), it has also created "the wretched of the earth," "the untouchables," and "the castaways" through various forms of oppression and exploitation. The institutions responsible for these forms of oppression and exploitation are what I call colonial apparatuses, which undermine the colony and colonized to a status of disorder and mimicry. These apparatuses become agents of power and subjectification reducing the colonized to powerless objects whose futile acts result into betrayal, playacting, corruption, and failure. This chapter explores the nature and scope of colonial apparatuses such as the colony, education, city, women, and politics, in order to understand Ralph Singh's shipwreck. Demonstration of Singh's pattern of movement from disorder to "playacting to disorder" to playacting (*Mimic Men* 184) and the role of colonial apparatuses in the creation and furtherance of his mimicry and disorder are essential to this understanding.

The colony, Isabella, is a major colonial apparatus. As a fictional island for the historical occurrences in the Caribbean, especially Trinidad and Guyana,[3] and a British colony pursuing independence, it reflects the rich mixture of African, Asian, and European heritages. Isabella also has a history of plantation economy, slavery, indentureship, and colonization, and the larger percentage of population is split between the Blacks and Indians (Hassan 1).[4] With a past of slavery and a present of colonization, Isabella, like many other colonies, becomes what Albert Memmi calls "a diseased society." Memmi explains that a "colonized society is a diseased society in which internal dynamics no longer succeed in creating new structures. Its century-hardened face has become nothing more than a mask under which it slowly smothers and dies. Such a society," Memmi continues, "cannot dissolve the conflicts of generations, for it is unable to be transformed" (99). "A diseased society" produces fragmented and displaced characters who express their disorder through escapism or violence. Richard Wright and James T. Farrell have convincingly depicted how a diseased society, the city of Chicago, molds Bigger Thomas and Studs Lonigan, twists and makes them killers, and then kills them (Deena, "The Irrationality of Bigger Thomas' World" 26-27).

Built upon the genocide of the Amerindians,[5] enslavement of the people of African decent, and indentureship of Asians, Isabella has become a poor, confining, and exploited society. It has already inherited disorder from the colonizer. Ralph Singh acknowledges the reality that "to be born in an island like Isabella, an obscure New World, transplantation, second hand and barbarous, was to be born to disorder" (118), while the inhabitants from a similar colonial society gladly, but regretfully, escape. G., the narrator of In the Castle of My Skin, becomes anxious to escape San Cristobal, fictional Barbados and Caribbean, but he regrets "seeing things for the last time ....people, objects, situations," because he realizes that he "had said farewell to the land" (300-03). Miguel Street's narrator also flees this limited/limiting society with the realization that colonial exploitation has stunted his own psychological and spiritual growth: "I left them all and walked briskly towards the aeroplane, not looking back, looking only at my shadow before me, a dancing dwarf on the tarmac" (222). Singh prepares to leave Isabella with great expectation, since he feels he will leave his disorder—his past, his secrets, school and unreality, a lack of history, his father's escape and eccentricity, and his Uncle Cecil's extravagance and destruction. But Singh experiences regret after refusing to go with Hok to the restaurant (179), for on the ship he realizes the depth of his alienation and pain as he remembers their "last family lunch" arranged by his father and as he reads Hok's unsigned typewritten message: "Some day we shall meet, and some day" (180). Commenting on the need to escape the limitations of a colony, Lamming claims that the Caribbean writers "simply had to get out of the place where they were born," lest they die psychologically, like Roger Mais (Pleasures of Exile 41). Therefore, both writers and characters from the colonies have been seriously affected by limitation and escapism.

The first phase of Ralph Singh's life in the colony reflects his displacement during childhood, before leaving for England. Discovering his displacement and disorder, Singh responds to them. He also escapes from displacement and disorder, but with them. This phase and place record Singh's childhood, adolescence and initiation into manhood, his many secrets, his colonial education that reinforces the lack of history and reality, and his conflict of dealing with paradoxes. Numerous conflicts arise from the double standards of school, the oppositional perspective between the blacks and Indians, the secrets of escape and shipwreck, and the disagreement between his father's poverty and his mother's rich family. Robert Morris illustrates Singh's disorder through paradoxes on Isabella:

> For Singh, son of a poor school teacher, though allied on his mother's side to the millionaire-owner of the Bella Bella Coca-Cola Bottling Plant, the island is a place of paradox of tensions. He is fascinated by wealth and poverty alike; he is drawn to his rich cousin Cecil and to the less rich, but more aristocratic creole family of the Deschampsneufs; yet he is also attracted to the struggling ambitious blacks like Hok and Browne. Like them he loathes the daily "betrayals into ordinariness," cherishes their secret dreams of escape from Isabella, and dreams himself, inflamed by his reading The Aryan People and Their Migrations, of fulfilling the prophecy incarnate in his surname. (61)

The paradox between the "poor school teacher" and the "millionaire" mother's family secures for Singh's father "the engaging reputation of a bottle-breaker and cafe-wrecker," makes "him into a type of eccentric squire" and "radical," and forces him into escapism and eccentricity (119). In addition, Singh's father's repetition of sentences, out of context laughter, "absurd questions," "fixed, ugly grin" (119), obsession with pornography (101), and religious escapism from his "deep distress" (128) become "disquieting" and "fatiguing" to Singh (119). He interprets "these religious excesses...as an attempt to deny the general shipwreck," but they "generated anger ....comradeship ....disorder," and self-delusion (127). So drama[6] added to disorder brings further mimicry and leaves the colonized people in a state of total dependency on drama (127).

At the center of Ralph Singh's mimicry is a growing sense of alienation and displacement. Secrets accumulate in his life and enhance further drama, but disturbance of the secrets and invasion of the private by the public increase alienation (131). Singh's secrets, of his father's pornographic pictures (101), of his suspicion that "between Cecil and one of his sisters there existed an incestuous relationship" (123), of his father's religion (125), of his father's connection with the sacrificial killing of Deschampsneufs' horse, Tamango (140), of Browne and Deschampsneufs' secret, private worlds (144), of his father's son, Dalip, and debt of thirty dollars (161–62), of his dream of sucking his mother's breasts (116), of his name, of "being marked" (94), and of the whispered word, "wife," to his teacher's ear (90), inflate the dramatic as "secrets add to secrets, weight to weight" (116). But "the camera ....in the sky" (116) facilitates the invasion of his private world by the "outside world," thus publicizing his privacy like the "opening" of "a letter" (148). Singh recalls the pain and burden of his childhood secrets:

> But childhood was for me a period of incompetence, bewilderment, solitude and shameful fantasies. It was a period of burdensome secrets—like the word "wife", a discovery about the world which I was embarrassed to pass on to the world—and I longed for nothing so much as to walk in the clear air of adulthood and responsibility, where everything was comprehensible and I myself was as open as a book. I hated my secrets. A complying memory has obliterated many of them and edited my childhood down to a brief cinematic blur. Even this is quite sufficiently painful. (90)

Forced to move in with their mother's family, Singh's family experiences a new alienation and displacement. Singh grows increasingly away from his family, and even his final attempt to reconnect with his father, on the eve of his departure, results in failure (176-77). He enters Deschampsneufs and Browne's worlds "tremulously and unwilling," but in so doing, he disrupts their secrets and they too begin to drift apart in mimicry (144). This disruption eventually makes Singh "a prisoner" of his "relationship with Browne, that understanding which began, continued and faded away in misunderstanding. A burdensome relationship, a boyhood uneasiness." Therefore, he needs "an alien witness to prove his reality" (187-88). Fear of exposure of each other's past fosters a certain "uneasiness" and distance, and through mimicry, they attempt to escape the past, rather than confront it. Thus, the postcolonial politics of Isabella originates from the rubble of drama and disorder (188-89). (I will pursue this point later, in my discussion of politics as another colonial apparatus).

Ralph Singh also grows away from his school friends, like his refusal to go out with Hok to the restaurant (179-80), and from his community. And these elements of uprootedness maim Ralph Singh, "imbue him with intimations of power ....shatter his foundation of family and stability ....desensitize him to pity ....make him retrench further into the role of observer in order to avoid further wounding" (Morris 61), and reinforce his resolution "to abandon the shipwreck island and all on it" (118), since he associates "disorder" and "placelessness" of his youth with Isabella (154).

In the first phase of Ralph Singh's colonized life, the nature and scope of his shipwreck become further enlarged and complicated through the creation of unrealistic myth and his inability to distinguish between reality and unreality. Through a carefully crafted colonial education system, the second colonial apparatus of power, the colonizer prepares the colonized for a role of unquestionable service.[7] And in so doing, colonial education further alienates and fragments the already ruptured child. King suggests that "at school the children are prepared to be mimic men of the New World" (78). George Lamming, Wole Soyinka, V. S. Naipaul, R. K. Narayan, and other postcolonial writers have illustrated, in their fiction and criticism, the growing displacement and fragmentation of students in a colony. Colonial education makes Lakunle, a Westernized school teacher, a pathetic and confused figure of mimicry which causes his loss of Sidi, the Belle (Soyinka, *The Lion and the Jewel*). It also alienates G from his friends—Bob, Boy Blue, and the gang. Boy Blue explains that "you never know as you yourself say when something go off pop in your head an you ain't the same man you think you wus" (Lamming, *In the Castle of My Skin* 142). King supplements that "the second exile is brought about through education and reading. Singh's lack of wholeness, of identity and authenticity, leads to his posturing, dandyism and flight into exile" (*V. S. Naipaul* 78).

From the fragmented perspective colonial education has created in Ralph Singh, his intellect becomes fascinated with anything from overseas, but Isabella depresses him. Singh's reaction to snow records the incongruity of his education: "Snow. At last, my element. And these were the flakes, the airiest crushed ice" (6). Bruce MacDonald sees Singh's reaction as "rather strange for someone who has lived his life on a tropical island" (249). But this and other incidents, referred to later, indicate the damaging effects of Singh's colonial education. In brief, it creates, as the epigram indicates, "schizophrenia" or "mimicry" (Naipaul, *An Area of Darkness* 56–57).

Singh's first memory of school indicates the extent of his colonial rupture. He remembers taking an apple to the teacher, but Isabella has no apples, yet his "memory insists on the apple" (90). In his puzzlement, his fragmented consciousness explains that "the editing is clearly at fault, but the edited version is all" he has (90). Vivek Dhaershwar attributes Singh's puzzlement to the effects of colonial education in which the school is seen "as a site of Subjectification" (75). He postulates that in the process of "subjectification," Singh's "identity is produced by the kind of asymmetrical power implied in the substitution of the "apple" for the "orange"—the "metropolitan" object/practice for the colonial one" (75). Such colonial rupture has added another dimension of disorder to Singh's consciousness, and it has done this by "the menace of mimicry" or "double vision which in disclosing ambivalence of colonial discourse," it "disrupts its authority" (Bhabha, "Of Mimicry and Men" 129).

The colonial education builds unrealism, illusion, and mimicry of what the students are and what they should be, of the private and public, and of the internal and external. The school fosters such dichotomy through its "secrets," imposition of British curriculum on the colony, and creation of the view that "everyday life" is an embarrassment. At the latter, the students laugh, but return to it daily. Peter Nazareth's comments provide further insights into the basis for such a conflicting behavior: "A colonized people, having lost its culture and believing that 'culture' always comes from the Mother Country, has a psychological need to feel that the world it lives in and the life it leads are real and worthy of art" ("*Mimic Men* as Study of Corruption" 93).[8]

The teacher's effort to deal with the ambivalence he has helped to create in his students becomes a hypocritical action of pretense, since he operates as a colonial agent under the principal and the British school inspector. Unconscious of his pawn-like role in the whole process of subjectification, in which students live double lives, the teacher becomes preoccupied with cure rather than prevention. The incident with Hok reveals both irony and tragedy of the teacher's role. The students and their teacher are marching in a "crocodile" to the Training College to provide practice for the student-teachers. Hok, a mixture of Chinese, European or Syrian, and African, denies his mother on the basis of race. His refusal to acknowledge his mother causes the procession to stop. The teacher orders him to greet his mother, but he only responds swiftly after the teacher threatens him with a tamarind rod. Hok returns crying, and Singh makes an important connection with Hok:

> It was for this betrayal that I knew he was crying. It was at this betrayal that the brave among us were tittering. It wasn't only that the mother was black and of the people, though that was a point; it was that he had been expelled from that private hemisphere of fantasy where lay his true life. The last book he has been reading was *The Heroes*. What a difference between the mother of Perseus and that mother! What a difference between the white, blue and dark green landscapes he had so recently known and that street! Between the street and the Chinese section of the Carnegie Library; between that placid shopping mother and the name of Confucius her son had earned among us for his wit and beauty. I felt that I had been given an unfair glimpse of another person's deepest secrets. I felt on that street, shady, with gardens, and really pretty as I now recall it, though then to me wholly drab, that Hok had dreams like mine, was probably also marked, and lived in imagination far from us, far from the island on which he, like my father, like myself, had been shipwrecked. (97)

Gareth Griffith's statement accurately sums up the role of the school. Griffith points out that "colonial educational policies were directed towards the suppression of a sense of identity" (83). This "suppression of a sense of identity" dislocates and disorients the colonized. Singh's dream of broken legs and the "terrors of arithmetic" connects his fractured identity in the city with the school:

> I dreamt that in this city I was being carried helplessly down a swiftly flowing river, the Thames, that sloped, and could only break my fall by guiding my feet to the concrete pillars of the bridge that suddenly spanned the river, and in my dream I felt the impact and knew that I had broken my legs and lost their use forever—but as in a dream, I say, the terrors of arithmetic disappear. And I am in a new school. (91)

The image of "the fractured personality, the spiritual cripple" (Lyn 62), is with Singh on the colony, grows with him in school, and goes with him to London: "I wish then to go back as whole as I had come ....the world continues over private fabrication, departure is departure. It fractures; the bone has to be set anew each time" (180). A "fractured personality" in a fractured society results in greater disorder, and playacting further complicates the shipwreck because "such a society understandably has no inner values. It merely copies its way of life from the Western Consumer society, 'B' films, and cheap American [London] magazines. It is dazzled by the glitter of luxuries" (Nazareth 86). This feature of Caribbean colonial society is well illustrated by contemporary musicians like *The Trade Winds*. The lyrics of their song, "It's Traditional," juxtapose the colonized's flexibility in acculturalization through copying the dominant culture against the colonizer's rigidity in the preservation of his culture and resistance to the colonized's culture. Thus, Singh's response to his ruptured culture, personality, and identity is "not to simplify but to complicate" (93), and therein lies his escapism. By a process of deconstruction, he copies and complicates Deschampsneufs' name. Taking a pattern from the French name, he breaks "Kirpalsingh into two, correctly reviving an ancient fracture" (93), thereby giving himself R. R. K. Singh.

Irrelevancy and derogation filter through colonial education to dehumanize the students. While Deschampsneufs—of European origin—receives special treatment from the teacher and impresses everyone with his wealth, Browne and Singh cover-up their fragmentation with mimicry. Major Grant's derogatory name calling of "Blue-cart Brown," to prophecy Browne's future career as garbage-collector, receives aggressive and retreating mimicry from Browne and Singh, respectively. Browne bangs the desk lid when the teacher tries to poke fun at Singh's father (130–31), excels at mimicry with his song "Oh, I'm a happy little nigger," and inflates the master's joke about Browne's lateness (130–31). Singh's mimicry, on the other hand, withdraws and retreats. His private deconstruction of his name mitigates "the fantasy or deception" (93). He eats his collar, reads strange books (95), imitates the older athletes (114), embraces his Aryan ancestry (102), and resolves to migrate (118). Singh explains the process of his withdrawal or retreat as the passing of time. He claims that "we cannot keep ourselves back for some tract of life ahead. We are made by everything, by action, by withdrawal ....But my failure was my silence. I was silent ....The true embarrassment, I could see, was my presence in the class" (132–33).

In *The Enigma of Arrival*, Naipaul further describes this colonial education as "abstract education":

And how could my knowledge of the world not be abstract, when all the world I knew at the age of eighteen was the small colonial world of my little island in the mouth of the Orinoco, and within that island the world of my family, within our little Asian-Indian community: small world within small world. I hardly knew our own community; of other communities I knew even less. I had no idea of history—it was hard to attach something as grand as history to our island. I had no idea of government. I knew only about a colonial governor and executive council and a police force. So that almost everything I read about history and other societies had an abstract quality. I could relate it only to what I knew: every kind of reading committed me to fantasy. (143)

Naipaul's colonial education is limited and it limits. Its "abstract quality" enhances Singh's knowledge of Europe, but denies him a sense of his own history, thereby leaving him ignorant of essential preparation for the confrontation of his disorder. Dhareshwar claims that "this education does not simply leave him [Singh] ignorant about his island and its community: it disengages him from them by subjecting him to a stereotypical knowledge about them, by devaluating his local knowledge of his community." Dhareshwar further explains that "the process of dissociating oneself from family and the community, the attempt to 'disentangle oneself from the camouflage of people,' goes hand in hand with the desire for a 'fresh start,' for the romance of life in the metropolis" (92).

Colonial society, with its economic and political systems, has fractured the spiritual and moral wholeness of Ralph Singh, but education advances his 'fracture' to the point of 'hollowness' and mimicry.[9] Singh links the effects of his education to the irrelevancy of the books and materials: "We, here on our island, handling books printed in this world...had been abandoned and forgotten. We pretended to be real, to be learning, to be preparing ourselves for life, we mimic men of the new world...with all its reminders of the corruption that came so quickly to the new" (146). In a similarly sweeping statement, MacDonald sums up the shipwrecking effects of colonial education on Singh's disorder and mimicry: "The apples, the snow, and the traffic jams in Liège were of the 'true pure world' from which came the text books, customs, ideas, and languages which were taught in the schools of Isabella. The children attempted to imitate what they learned, to be real in the sense that the books prescribed." MacDonald further indicates that "the children also attempted to deny their own world: 'The laughter denied our knowledge of these things to which after the hours of school we were to return' (114)" (249-50).

The third colonial apparatus, the city of London, plays a role of enhancing and complicating Singh's disorder and mimicry. The city promises the illusion of order, but it rewards a greater disorder by forcing upon the lonely Londoners a new but sophisticated displacement, alienation, racism, bewilderment, and corruption (Selvon, *The Lonely Londoners*). Singh records how he has been deceived by "the great city, the centre of the world, in which, fleeing disorder," he "had hoped to find the beginning of order," since "so much had been promised by the physical aspect" (18). According to Lendeg White, "it is the colonial myth that London is the centre of the world that first defines his sense of shipwreck on the island" (164), which Singh celebrates upon his arrival in London: "Here was the city, the world. I waited for the flowering to come to me. The trams on the Embankment sparked blue. The river was edged and pierced with reflections of light, blue and red and yellow. Excitement!" (18). But Singh quickly and painfully discovers the emptiness and elusiveness of the city. The city's "heart must have lain somewhere," "the god of the city was elusive," the "factories and warehouses" of the city "were empty and fraudulent," and each individual has returned "to his own cell...in this solid city" where "life was two-dimensional" (18-19). White elaborates on the implications of the "shrinking of London to a two-dimensional city:" "Instead of a London which offers an escape from colonial disorder, we have a London which underlines that disorder more acutely than ever before" (164).

The city quickly grows sour for Singh. In seeking "the physical city," he finds "only a conglomeration of private cells" (18). Most colonized, marginalized, and oppressed people gravitate to large cities in pursuit of freedom, escapism, and, or, opportunities. However, many, like Ralph Singh, V. S. Naipaul, George Lamming, Samuel Selvon, and his characters in *The Lonely Londoners* share similar experiences with that of Richard Wright. His "dream of going North and writing books, novels ....symbolized to" him all he "had not felt and seen," and "by imagining a place where everything was possible," he "kept hope alive" (*Black Boy* 186). However, his "first glimpse of that flat black stretch of Chicago depressed and dismayed" him and "mocked all" his "fantasies" (*American Hunger* 1).[10]

Singh's moment of disappointment with London is described by Mac-Donald as "the moment of epiphany failed." MacDonald further explains that Singh's escape to London is "in order to end his feeling of placelessness and disorder; he expected the ritual of snow to unite him with his imagined cultural roots. He thought that only he was lost, that his society alone lacked unity; he did not realize that this was the universal condition of man in the twentieth century." MacDonald adds that "the moment of epiphany failed—Ralph was returned to reality in the same way that he had returned from school to the reality of Isabella" (250). In fact, quite early in London, Singh discovers this "epiphany failed," for "looking out from that empty room with the mattress on the floor" he "felt all the magic of the city go away and had an intimation of the forlornness of the city and the people who lived in it" (7).

Arriving in London with his colonial baggage and with the disappearance of the eye of the camera (30), Singh becomes a victim of the metropolitan city where alienation replaces accountability and lostness is disguised in freedom. Singh attributes his disorder to the absence of a guide.[1] But Lieni fulfills the role of his guide. Lieni plays the game with him and accepts the role/character he has created. Furthermore, Lieni, "by suggestion and flattery, created the character of the rich colonial," and "sought merely to heighten" this created character (20).

In London, Singh tries to escape his disorder through playacting, but his efforts encounter failure. London,[12] an old deformed city, is filled with disorder, and the people who have come to live there, have become victims of its process of objectification. These fragmented objects, like Lieni, Beatrice, and others, seek to reverse their objectification, but in so doing, they spread the city's disorder to Singh. Moreover, London has been the source of colonial disorder in Isabella. Therefore, Singh has to find ways to deal with this greater disorder and with the "growing dissociation between" the inhabitants and "the city in which" they live separate lives. The inhabitants of London are "reduced, reciprocally, to a succession of such meetings," and their personalities are "divided bewilderingly into compartments" (27). However, Singh's problem is, "in seeking order, seeking the flowering, [and] the extension to" himself that should have come from the city, he "had tried to hasten a process which had seemed elusive" and he "had tried to give" himself "a personality," but he discovers that "each person concealed his own darkness" (26–27). Thus, in his "confused" and "faded" ambition, he longs "for the certainties of ....Isabella, certainties which" he "once dismissed as shipwreck" (27).

In his various attempts to escape his shipwreck, Ralph Singh connects with his Aryan past (MacDonald 25), and this connection forms another connection—the city and sex. Singh illustrates "how right" his "Aryan ancestors were to create gods." He continues, "We seek sex, and are left with two private bodies on a stained bed. The larger erotic dream, the god, has eluded us. It is so whenever, moving out of ourselves, we look for extensions of ourselves. It is with city as it is with sex. We seek the physical city and find only a conglomeration of private cells" (18). Singh's pursuit of sex with women shatters his fantasy through his numerous sexual failures which add to his disorder and playacting. The women—his mother, Lieni, Sandra, Wendy, and Isabella–, objects and exploits of colonization, influence his shipwreck.[13] Isabella, the colony, bears the name of queen Isabella who is at the center of Columbus' rediscovery of the New World, resulting in slavery and colonization. His mother represents colonial capitalism since her family "owned the Bella Bella Bottling Works and were among other things the local bottlers of Coca-Cola" (83). Her family's riches and extravagance despise and alienate Ralph's father, and set a pattern of elitism and displacement in the boy's life. Nazareth remarks that "the local capitalists of Isabella are nothing better than debris—agents for external capitalists" (82). Although Singh sympathizes with his father, he always identifies with his mother's family for fame, fear, and fun. His father hates Cecil (86), yet Ralph likes Cecil (101), "and between the middle-aged man and the young boy" he acts "as go between" (86). Even though Singh attributes the murder of his father to Cecil, in creating "the dande, the extravagant colonial," he associates with his mother's family and promotes his lineage as "the Bottlers of Coca-Cola" (20).

Lieni, Sandra, and Stella are major tools of colonial power and subjectification in Ralph Singh's life. An immigrant in London, Lieni brings her own colonial baggage, covers it with "the smart London girl" image (29), and merges it with Singh's disorder. This merger results in a dramatic creation and leads to further disorder. In the absence of the camera, Lieni becomes his guide. She selects his clothes, dresses him, and helps to create his new character of the "rich colonial" (20). Singh's statement, "we become what we see of ourselves in the eyes of others" (20), becomes an important aspect of building a new self-concept and character. For as Lieni dresses, approves, and sends him out to conquer, she expects him to bring back women to her boarding-house (21). Singh responds, "And because she expected me to do so, I did" (21). In fact, Singh becomes her apt pupil, her tool, and her agent to spread disorder through their mimicry. In the sexual exploitation of other women, Singh tries to be the subject, but his failures reduce him to further objectification of himself and his identity (28).[14] So he wears his mask, again, and escapes into cultural and linguistic alienation. He pursues sexual relationships with French, Norwegian, and Swedish girls whose languages separate them from any meaningful dialogue about his failure. This new strategy ushers disorder into his most sacred and intimate world: "Intimacy: the word holds the horror.... I was capable of the act required, but frequently it was in the way that I was capable of getting drunk or eating two dinners. Intimacy: it was violation and self-violation" (25).

Ralph Singh's relationship with Sandra reveals a process of further degeneration since Sandra, too, has her baggage of disorder. In the headquarters of colonization, London, several factors force disorder on Sandra. These include Sandra's repeated quarrels with her father (42), failure of passing a qualifying exam for the second time, the end of her government grant, the end of school, no degree, and no escape by route (46). Subsequently, Sandra and Singh's marriage is built on the pillar of disorder. Viney Kirpal argues that the "foundations" of this relationship "are predicated entirely in sensual, sexual, romantic terms." Kirpal further links "Singh's infatuation" with "the native's colonial obsession with the white woman/Britain. Her provocative animality and ruggedness attract and excite him," but leave him obsessed with "body-oriented and physical" language (53). He is fascinated with her "curving and rounded...breasts which in their free state alter their shape and contour...breasts which in the end madden the viewer" (43). Fanon's psychological and postcolonial theory illuminates the nature of "the native's colonial obsession with the white woman/Britain." He observes that the man of color's attempt at decolonization reveals intricate psychological and racial dynamics:

> Out of the blackest part of my soul, across the zebra striping of my mind, surges this desire to be suddenly *white*. I wished to be acknowledged not as *black* but as *white*. Now...who but a white woman can do this for me? By loving me she proves that I am worthy of white love. I am loved like a white man. I am a white man. Her love takes me onto the noble road that leads to total realization.... I marry white culture, white beauty, white whiteness. When my restless hands caress those white breasts, they grasp white civilization and dignity and make them mine. (*Black Skin* 63)

Sandra's obsession with her breasts expresses her emotional and spiritual disorder. Singh points out that "no one loved her breasts more than Sandra herself. She caressed them in moments of abstraction; and indeed it was this ritualistic, almost Pharaonic, attitude—right hand supporting and caressing left breast, left hand supporting right—which had first brought her to my startled if delighted attention" (43-44). Fleeing from her family dislocation, Sandra meets Singh (43), and complicates his shipwreck by almost ordering him to propose marriage to her (46). Societal and Sandra's expectation of action from Singh forces him to act, but he also reacts and playacts. He is also acted upon. Recognizing his depressive mood, Sandra, who "had been endlessly passive, accepting all strokings and kissings as part of a rightful homage," now "offered" Singh "her painted breasts," and "she made an effort to take the lead" by pressing her breasts to all parts of his body (48). This erotic awakening in Singh's fantasy with Sandra's breasts drives him into heightened sexual disorder where, after his fascination with breasts, he can only relate to a woman's body in a disgusting and grotesque manner. Three years later he can still see the prostitute's breasts as "enormous...grotesque, empty starved sacks," her legs with "liquid folds" of flesh, and her "liquescent flesh," as "striped, indented, corrugated," and tormenting (236).

Although Singh's sexual disorder has its origin in Isabella, through Singh's exposure to his father's pornography (101) and his dream of fantasy with his mother's breasts (116), it increases in London, especially with Sandra. But his sexual failures in London addict him to a continuation of sexual disorder on his return to Isabella, where he "had become acquainted with a number of women of various races" (72). And at the climax of his sexual disorder, mimicry blinds his heart and eyes to a greater disorder, the break up of his marriage. After a sexually extravagant afternoon, as he mimics "darling, I've had a most marvelous afternoon. I've been in bed with a most skilled and delightful woman," he realizes that Sandra might have the same experience, and he is "amazed" at his "innocence" (72). Gloria Lyn points out that "marriage to Sandra is but a coupling of two castaways. Their experiences on Isabella reveal them to be social and cultural misfits in a society that is sick and confused" (59).

But two displaced, alienated, fractured, and disoriented individuals, from a dislocated city, in holy matrimony, grow farther apart on Isabella. The meeting with Singh's mother sets the stage for another dimension of displacement. Culturally, Sandra and her mother-in-law drift apart. Kirpal enumerates that while Sandra "'crosses the threshhold' geographically," by accompanying Singh from England to Isabella, she is "unprepared for the effort it takes to comprehend an unfamiliar world." Kirpal continues, "Her resolve to 'meet strange and ancient customs halfway' does not suffice because it is limited to the typical arrogance of the European estimating traditional societies in convenient stereotypes" (56). Sandra's drift away from her husband and mother-in-law parallels Singh's drift away from his wife and mother. In utter estrangement, Singh creates a society (Crippleville, the ruptured version of Kripalville) in a society (Isabella), and the former separates them from the wider community of the latter. Singh describes the nature of Crippleville and its exclusion:

> We were a haphazard, disordered, and mixed society in which there could be nothing like damaging exclusion; and before the end of that first fortnight we had found ourselves attached to the neutral, fluid group which was to remain ours for the next five or six years. The men were professional, young, mainly Indian, with a couple of local whites and coloured; they had all studied abroad and married abroad; on Isabella they were linked less by their background and professional standing than by their expatriate and fantastically cosmopolitan wives or girl friends. (55)

Singh and Sandra further drift apart because the old colonizer-colonized relationship produces "fear of place," sleeping in separate bedrooms, and barrenness as seen in both *Mimic Men* and *Wide Sargasso Sea*.[15] Kirpal asserts that "estrangement, the obverse of assimilation or true 'marriage,' occurs because of the inability of the white race to treat the coloured races as equals, as partners in a contract. Overtones of the historical master-slave relationship, in the form of racial arrogance, reasserts itself. The fear of being swamped by the inferior culture of the ex-slaves moves in the 'masters' a fierce desire to preserve themselves from the perilous onslaught" (55).

On Singh's second trip to London, as a politician, he encounters more dehumanization and manipulation. Crushed and utterly defeated by Lord Stockwell's colonial superiority and his full knowledge of Singh's father, Singh escapes in the city, because his reality has been shattered. He courts the "phantasy" of the city through his relationship with several women, including Lady Stella. As with Lieni and Sandra, Lady Stella wields colonial power through her recreation of the fantasy of the city, her substantial financial interest in Isabella, her use of nursery rhymes, and her sexual dominance. She forces him to read nursery rhymes, and Singh complies since "it was her theory that understanding was impossible between people who had not read the same children's books or heard the same nursery rhymes" (227). She also dictates their love-making, which Singh describes as "standardized." But later, he explains that their sexual relationship "was divided into two parts. The first was dedicated to me; the second Stella claimed for herself. For the first part she lay on her side and was passive. For the second she straddled me... she was all motion" (231). But the "speechless, prolonged second part was torment and torture" for Singh who seeks escapism in the reading of a book (232).

While Ralph Singh, the colonized, represents "decadence, moral degeneration and a preoccupation with the materialistic and the carnal," the European women represent different sides of Britain, the colonizer (Kirpal 86-87). Additionally, his "obsession (with England's perfection)" deceives "him into abandoning his own 'pure' beloved mother country and coming to serve the inferior, self-seeking, libertine English woman/England" (86-87). Kirpal further illustrates that "in the portraits, England is Sandra consumed by self-love and egotism...Stella the aristocrat, exhausted by ennui and left jaded by the persistent quest of pleasure and megalomanic self centeredness,...and the poor London prostitute" is "another face of the country—tragic, nauseating, grotesque, revolting, diseased." So the women/England/colonial exploit Singh/Isabella/colonized since they are active and aggressive, rather than passive (86-88).

Colonialism, with the aid of colonial education, trains the natives to be dependent on the colonizer who in turn declares the natives unfit to rule their own countries.[16] A century and more of this displacing and dehumanizing system leaves the colonized politicians in a state of mimicry, without real power, or as "hollow men" (Eliot, "Hollow Men").[17] Singh illustrates how the fifth colonial apparatus, colonial politics, further dehumanizes him:

> The pace of colonial events is quick, the turnover of leaders rapid ....The career of the colonial politician is short and ends brutally. We lack order. Above all, we lack power, and we do not understand that we lack power. We mistake words and acclamation of words for power; as soon as our bluff is called we are lost. Politics for us are a do-or-

die, once-for-all charge. Once we are committed we fight more than political battles; we often fight quite literally for our lives. Our transitional or makeshift societies do not cushion us. There are no universities or city houses to refresh us and absorb us after the heat of battle. For those who lose, and nearly everyone in the end loses, there is only one course: flight. Flight to the greater disorder, the final emptiness: London and the home counties. (8)

Politicians, on the whole, are hollowed people who cling to some form of artificial power to create the illusion of success through manipulation. Singh argues that while engineers have "concrete gifts," politicians have abstract gifts. They "make something out of nothing ....They are manipulators...they seldom know what they seek" because they are "driven by some little hurt, some little incompleteness" (37). They become fearful and insecure since they only have "the trappings of power" (191), and the fear of losing this abstract power drives them to create drama (192). At the Roman House,[18] Singh and Browne develop a court, a reproduction of the colonizer's world, with "competition to serve" and "murder in the wings." They embark on large scale military defense and security to heighten the drama. Singh points out that "with the court there came drama. Drama created itself around us. When reports came to us of violence, in various districts, the protection around the house increased" (195). But this large scale mimicry blinds them to their own playacting (191), and endangers their abstract, artificial power because they fail to see that power obtained easily will depart in the same manner (38). The tragedy of the colonial politician, therefore, is that "there is no way down. There can only be extinction. Dust to dust; rags to rags; fear to fear" (40).

Ralph Singh's colonial past; childhood in the colony, Isabella; colonial education; the great city of colonization, London; and sexual experience with European women have filled his mind with a cinematic dandyism. This type of mimicry denies him the knowledge and consciousness of the nature and scope of racial distress in politics and the truth about the colonizer's role in manipulating colonial political power. In the first case, Singh and Browne, representatives of the two major ethnic groups, have access to each other's boyhood secrets. This knowledge replaces the role of the camera and guide, signals betrayal, and reinforces further playacting. Singh becomes aware that "at any moment Browne might refer to" his "past," while Browne avoids any conversation about his boyhood of "Joe Louis, Haile Selassie, Jesus, that black jackass, the comic boy-singer" (188–89). Browne and Singh never confront their past. Rather, they cover-up their past and continue mimicking in their political careers. Singh adds to "the peculiar power of" his "name," the "reputation as a dandy...as a young ʹIsabella millionaireʹ who ʹworked hard and played hard,ʹ" while Browne adds his "licensed status as a renegade and romantic, a ʹradicalʹ,

for whose acknowledged gifts our island provided no outlet" (189). Political mimicry, therefore, renders them incapable of dealing with racial and political upheavals. Nazareth stresses that "the people [of Isabella] were lacerated by class and race differences before political activities began" (81). Unprepared and unable to cope with the "deep racial wounds," they escape into the mimicry of nationalization: "Nationalization had become a word" of mimicry and escapism to deal with the burning of sugar-cane fields, overrunning of police stations, looting of houses and shops, and the increase of racial disturbances (220).

Furthermore, "when the organized violence began ....men distraught with anger and fear and outrage ....when these men, braving the city streets, came to me at the Roman house with tales of Asiatic distress, of women and children assaulted, of hackings, of families burnt alive in wooden houses, I closed my eyes and thought about the horsemen riding to the end of the world" (241). Singh's abstract response to concrete tragedy is a direct result of his abstract colonial education and his shipwreck. Singh can only offer mental and psychological escapism since that has been his experience: "I said, 'Think about this as something in a book, in a newspaper. Do not give me names. Do not tell me how people died. Say instead, "Race riots occurred". Say, "There was loss of life"'" (241). Similarly, Singh offers the "comfort he offered" himself to the "poor man" who "had brought a stone stained and sticky with blood and fine hair, the hair perhaps of a child," hoping "to destroy the images of vulnerable flesh" (241). MacDonald finds Singh's "political career ....much like his father's. They became the heroes who could reinstitute in Isabella the ritual which could absolve the islanders of the responsibility of their own actions and at the same time give their acts a universal significance" (251–52).

In the second case, colonial politicians become puppets manipulated by colonizers through the queen's representative, the Governor and an elite group of 'lower class turned upper class' Europeans. Caught between the demands of the distressed people of Isabella and the tough, bureaucratic political-game of the colonizers, colonial politicians have to offer drama rather "than release from bitterness" (196). In utter powerlessness, they "used borrowed phrases which were part of the escape from thought, from that reality"; they "wanted people to see but could" themselves "scarcely face" (198). And in the creation of this inflated illusion, the wild men of Singh's party "promised to abolish poverty in twelve months...abolish bicycle licences...discipline the police...intermarriage...higher prices for sugar and copra and cocoa...and to nationalize every foreign-owned estate" (199).

As a further empty pretentiousness of this dramatic illusion, the colonial politicians frenzily embark on several dramatic games. They play the "game of naming," naming documents, statements, buildings, roads, and agricultural schemes (214-15). They "cut ribbons across brief stretches of country road," open "laundries, shoe-shops, and filling stations," photograph politicians "shaking hands with the representatives of a French motorcar firm," and attach themselves "to all the activity of the island and to whatever...passed for industrialization or investment" (215). For these politicians, drama "reinforced reality. It reinforced that sense of ownership" (215), which is what they pursue in nationalization.

Nevertheless, Singh's ultimate shipwreck is registered with the culmination of all the apparatuses of colonial power—the colonizer, the mystic city of London with its magical light (224), women like Lady Stella reinforcing dominance and enhancing Singh's continued sexual failure, reminder of colonial education through Stella's insistence on Singh's memorization of nursery rhymes and fairy stories in place of *The Aryan Peoples and Their Migrations* (227), and the crown of colonial power, Lord Stockwell. Stockwell's repeated denial of Singh's petition for nationalization and independence finally deflates his inflated mimicry. Disappointment and disillusionment drive Singh to flirt with "needed new sights, new landscapes, and unfamiliar language" of the city (233). But this escape cannot rid him of his personal, political, and sexual failures. Rather, his colonial octopus engulfs, crushes, and leaves him with "images of shipwreck, dissolution, drifting, crippling deformities, isolation and alienation" (Lyn 65); "incompetence, bewilderment, solitude, shameful fantasies" (90); and images of death, decay (152-53), and castaway (106). And in "a massive, contradictory but satisfying case made against" him, his disorder and mimicry are summed up in his "private life...methodical making of money...racial exclusiveness of [the] development of Crippleville...marriage to Sandra...relationship with Wendy...escapade with Stella...sold out on the nationalization issue...[and] playboy attitude to distress" (238). At the extremity of his colonial shipwreck, Singh, in exile outside London, seeks new opportunities through writing. For Singh, writing "clarifies and even becomes a process of life" (231), yet one wonders about his new freedom and his ability to confront the past—of colonial disorder and mimicry—with the arrival of the guest of honor's wife, Lady Stella, at his hotel (251).

In brief, my argument postulates how colonization has created disorder and mimicry in Ralph's life, and Naipaul skillfully links Columbus' rediscovery of the West Indies in 1492 to the fracture of these colonies. Lyn emphasizes that "the mention of Columbus at the end of part one is a reminder that the island of Isabella represents the disorder and upheaval that are a consequence of the voyages of discovery" (62).[19] Natives, like Ralph Singh, bewilderingly try to interpret their colonial fragmentation. They pursue meaning and significance from their shipwreck, but colonial apparatuses like Isabella, education, the city of London, European women, and politics frustrate their pursuit. The end results of colonization, therefore, are disorder and mimicry created through a cinematic juxtaposition between reality and illusion. Singh has been emasculated by colonization, and mimicry fails to free him from disorder, so he embraces decolonization through the writing of his analytical autobiography, which becomes an important tool for Singh, Naipaul, and all colonized peoples' emancipation. Eventually, Singh's writing project frees him from disorder and mimicry.

# Notes

1.  I am thinking about Paul's statement to the Philippians: "I count not myself to have apprehended: but this one thing I do, forgetting those things which are behind, and reaching forth unto those things which are before" (Phil. 3:13).

2.  The term is appropriated from Vivek Dhareshwar's "Self-fashioning, Colonial Habitus, and Double Exclusion: V. S. Naipaul's *The Mimic Men.*" Dhareshwar's use of the phrase "the school as one of the apparatuses of colonial power, as a site of subjectification" provides insight into my formulation and discussion of the various apparatuses of colonialism.

3.  Peggy Nightingale adds Jamaica to the list. She verifies that "Isabella, the island, is a fictional compilation of elements from Trinidad, Jamaica, and Guyana" (528).

4.  According to Hassan, Africans were captured and brought to the West Indies to solve the labor problem. The first batch of slaves arrived in the West Indies in 1672, and thereafter a steady flow of slaves were brought to the Caribbean through the "middle passage." In the Caribbean, slavery was abolished in 1833 and emancipated in 1838. These freed slaves abandoned the sugar estates in search of independent livelihood to better their conditions. This action created labor shortage, which the colonizers tried to solve by recruiting and indenturing Portuguese and Chinese, who failed to cope with labor conditions. So, by foul means Indians were indentured to solve the problem. Proving to be successful farmers, the Indians were further enticed or trapped to remain in the Caribbean. Hassan further points out that "Indian immigration, which started in 1838 in Guyana and 1845 in Trinidad, punctuated by intermittent breaks, was banned in 1917 because of strong criticisms from Mahatma Gandhi and other Indian leaders" (3-4).

5.  Europeans, the colonizers, "established a white obligarch with unlimited political and economic power over the rest of the population" (Hassan 3). Edgar Mittleholzer's works depict this crucial period of Caribbean history.

6.  "Amerindians" is the equivalent of "Native Americans," who have been destroyed and/or driven into the jungles of South America by the colonizers.

7.  "Drama" and "play-acting" are used interchangeably. They carry the meaning of unreality, insincerity, and theatrical performance.

8.  Chapter one of *Canonization, Colonization, Decolonization* explores the role of colonial education in the creation of class. It also illustrates how this education prepares the

natives for submissive service.  Chapter two explores the dehumanizing aspect of colonial education.

9.  Achebe Africanizes this point in the following manner: "If I were God I would regard as the very worst our acceptance—for whatever reason—of racial inferiority.  It is too late in the day to get worked up about it or to blame others, much as they may deserve such blame and condemnation.  What we need to do is to look back and try and find out where we went wrong, where the rain began to beat us" ("The Novelist as Teacher" 44).  Achebe illuminates his point with two examples.  He explains the "shock felt by Christians" of his "father's generation," in the "early forties when for the first time the local girls' school performed Nigerian dances at the anniversary of the coming of the gospel," since they had always put on European performances (44).  The other example describes a student who wrote about winter instead of "harmattan" so that the other boys would not laugh at him (44).

10.  T. S. Eliot's works, particularly "Hollow Men" and "The Love Song of J. Alfred Prufrock," are alluded to here.

11.  See Deena's "The Irrationality of Bigger Thomas's World" for a full discussion of Wright's anticipation of and disappointment with the city of Chicago (27–29).

12.  Although Singh claims that "in London" he "had no guide," who would "link" his "present to" his "past," one must recognize the irony of his self-delusion.  Singh indulges in an existentialist persona of creating and fulfilling his own role and character.  However, Singh remarks: "The respect with which I was treated from boys from the island ….was a help, as was Lieni's willingness to play the game. Lieni. I had no guide, I said; and so it seemed to me at that time. But there was Lieni in her basement" (20).

13.  London is part of the dark and hypocritical Europe, which has created Kurtz (Conrad 45).

14.  The women discussed, in this section, as a colonial apparatus are really victims of colonial exploitation.  However, since the focus of this discussion is Singh's victimization, these women are seen by Singh, and subsequently portrayed, as colonial agents.

15.  My use of the word "objectification" here depicts "that which is affected or intended to be affected by feeling or action."  I borrowed the grammatical use of the word "object," which receives the action of a verb, or "endures the effect of this action" (Funk & Wagnalls' definition of object).

16.  Kirpal explores several of these relationships in Third World literature.  He traces a pattern of "what begins in great passion, love, enchantment, usually wanes into disaffection, estrangement, separation..... As a first indication, the marriages are usually barren, childless, that is to say unproductive.  Sandra and Ralph Singh (*The Mimic Men*) have no children while Madeleine and Ramaswamy (*The Serpent and the Rope*) lose both theirs in disease or still birth.  Nicole is forced by Roger in (*Water With Berries*) to abort every child conceived.  Abdul and Odili in (*The Nowhere Man*) are issueless, whereas Srinivas and Mrs. Pikering are too aged to start a family.  Caroline and Valmiki (*Possession*) do not marry or set up a family.  Samba and

Lucienne in (*Ambiguous Adventure*) part company and do not marry. Irene and Padmanabha Tyer (*Comrade Kirillov*) are the only exception with two living children but the alienation between the couple also emerges fairly strong as the novel develops" (54). To this list of barren marriages/relationships, I would add Edward Rochester and Antoinnette Cosway (*Wide Sargasso Sea*) and the numerous relationships in (*The Lonely Londoners*) which end without marriage or children.

17. See the introduction of *Canonization, Colonization, Decolonization* for a discussion of the dependence theory. Albert Memmi, Philip Mason, and O. Mammoni advance this argument. But Mammoni argues that, once given the chance, all peoples have the ability to govern themselves.

18. Peter Nazareth's "'The Mimic Men' as a Study of Corruption" provides insightful connections between Eliot's "hollow men"/Prufrock and Ralph Singh/colonized politicians.

19. See Landeg White for an interesting exploration of Naipaul's treatment of "House." In *Miguel Street*, the house serves as the spot from which the street can be viewed, while in *The Mystic Masseur*, house is the image of a compromise, and *A House for Mr. Biswas* employs the use of house as a central unifying symbol. In *The Mimic Men*, there are a series of houses. Kripal Singh's house collapses, Browne's house is a racial prison, and the boarding house on Kensington, High Street is packed with imigrants and owned by a Jew. The Roman, Beach, and Scandinavian houses express expatriate taste, but none are homes. Neither do they contain order, light, beauty, and achievement. They are temporary residences of shipwrecked people (153-84).

   The following is the passage referred to: "I thought of Columbus....I thought of that world which, as I was steadily separated from it, became less and less discovered, less and less real" (180).

# Colonial Alienation Producing Madness in Jean Rhys' *Wide Sargasso Sea*

While the ultimate implications of that always–destructive colonial/imperial relation are now laid bare, so too are the very real similarities between Antoinette's fate and that of black slaves in European hands. Antoinette is bought for profit, and is regarded as exotic, hysterical, and incomprehensible by her buyer. He changes her name to a more comfortably English one, and she is dependent on him for her very existence. When she seems to show signs of rebellion she is cruelly punished, though the evidence against her is at best circumstantial. Finally she is reviled as a wild animal and confined in a cruelly uncongenial prison. Antoinette Cosway is thus shown to share the history, which apparently divided her from the Blacks. (Tiffin 338)

Alienation has become one of the most universal thematic explorations especially in the area of literature. H. A. Bulhan cites Geyer's bibliographical compilation of "1,800 books, articles, and dissertations on alienation" up to 1974. Much more has been written since then (185-86). Most critics and theorists of colonialism, including Marx and Fanon, recognize "the fact that alienation is central to any analysis of colonialism" (Joseph 7). Describing the role of language "in the colored man's comprehension of the dimension of *the other*," Fanon explains that "the black man has two dimensions. One with his fellows, the other with the white man. A negro behaves differently with a white man and with another negro. That this self-division is a direct result of colonialist subjugation is beyond question" (*Black Skin White Masks* 17). While Fanon took a psychological approach, championing "the wretched of the world: the colonized and their psychic disintegration," Marx took an economic approach to alienation, concerning "himself with the workers of the world: labor and its economic powerlessness" (Joseph 7). This chapter explores a postcolonial perspective of the theme of alienation in Jean Rhys' *Wide Sargasso Sea*. I shall demonstrate the implications of Antoinette's alienation, within the framework of colonialism.[1] My formulation of the theories of alienation emerges from a fusion of Marxist and Fanonian concepts,[2] and I will use the first four categories of Fanon's theories.

Bulhan has provided a brief, but useful, categorization of Marx's theory of alienation: "man's alienation from nature, man's alienation from himself, man's alienation from his species-being, and man's alienation from man" (186). Similar to, but different from the above categorization, Fanon's concept and formulation of his theory of alienation reflect influence from economics (Marx) and psychology. However, his emphasis is on culture and psychology. Emanuel Hansen confirms that Fanon's focus is on "the cultural and psychological forms of alienation of the colonized native" (80), while Bulhan summarizes Fanon's works on alienation in five categories: "alienation from the self, alienation from the significant other, alienation from the general other, alienation from one's culture, and alienation from creative social praxis" (188). Alienation from self, for Marx, means,

> 'estrangement from the things,' which means the alienation of the worker from the product of his labor—that is, the alienation of that which mediates his relation to the 'sensual external world' and hence to the objects of nature. What the worker produces is not his own, but rather someone else's; it meets not his own needs; it is a commodity he sells to eke out a bare existence. The more he produces, the more his product and hence the objects of nature stand opposed to him. (Bulhan 186)

Marx's influence can be traced in Fanon's concurrence that alienation is primarily economic: "If there is an inferiority complex, it is the outcome of a double process—primarily, economic;—subsequently, the internalization—or, better, the epidermalization—of this inferiority" (Fanon, Introduction to *Black Skin*, 11).

Economics, according to Rodney and Memmi, is at the center of colonization.[3] It is also the core of Antoinette Cosway/Mason/Rochester's tragedy. Margaret Paul Joseph's study of the importance of mirror as a reflection of otherness alludes to economic exploitation. Joseph argues that "the basis of the whole story is again a matter of economics...but wealth is turned into a major symbol of evil. Money is a corrupting influence and is linked to betrayal, revenge, and power." Continuing to illustrate how the power of money becomes the greatest evil, since money can ruin people's lives, Joseph advocates that "Annette Mason and Antoinette Cosway are both victims of Englishmen who, like countless others before them, went to the colonies to make money with no regard for the consequences on the lives of the people who lived there" (33-34).[4]

Gossiping ex-slaves perceptively point out that Mr. Mason "didn't come to the West Indies to dance—he came to make money as they all do. Some of the big estates are going cheap, and one unfortunate's loss is always a clever man's gain" (29-30).[5] As one of Antoinette's colonizer/Prospero, Mr. Mason's marriage to Annette sparks hostility from the ex-slaves. The marriage also leads to Antoinette's tragedy and alienation. Joseph explains that "the rich Mr. Mason (so sure of himself, so English in his confidence, thinks Antoinette) marries Mrs. Cosway and saves the estate they all love; but in true Prospero fashion he is insensitive to the mood of the laborers on the island and this brings tragedy to his wife and her children" (34). Failing to discern the ex-slaves' changing attitude, Mason assures Annette: "You were the widow of a slave-owner, the daughter of a slave-owner, and you had been living here alone, with two children, for nearly five years," but Annette perceptively points out her new economic status' influence on the exslaves: "We were so poor then...we were something to laugh at. But we are not poor now.... You are not a poor man. Do you suppose that they don't know all about your estate in Trinidad? And the Antigua property?" (32). Later, Antoinette interprets economics as the basis of her alienation: "The black people did not hate us quite so much when we were poor. We were white but we had not escaped and soon we would be dead for we had no money left. What was there to hate?" (34). Howells summarizes that Annette's "alliance with the new colonialism" sparks new implications (110), and Emery concurs that "Annette's marriage solidifies the power of the neocolonialists; it also intensifies the conflict between blacks and whites. The Blacks call them "White Cockroach," but the whites call them "white niggers" (102, 100). Whites alienate Annette's family on the basis of her low economic status, while blacks alienate them on the basis of her high economic status. Howells sums up this tragedy: "Hated by the blacks and despised for their poverty by both blacks and other whites, Antoinette and her mother are the victims of a system the collapse of which has not only dispossessed them as a class but also deprived them as individuals of any means of independent survival" (110).

Steeped in typical colonizer's overconfidence and arrogance, Mason's late-rescue-attempt is futile. Coulibri has been set on fire, Pierre, Antoinette's little retarded brother, is killed, Antoinette is hurt, and Annette goes mad. "Indirectly, Mason is the cause of her madness," claims Joseph, but he also causes Antoinette's displacement and alienation (35). Robbed of her mother, brother, stepfather, Tia, Christophine, and Coulibri, Antoinette is placeless.

After her recuperation at Aunt Cora's house, Antoinette is placed in a convent, "a place of...death" (56), where she prays "for a long time to be dead" (57).

Unaware of and unconcerned about his role in Annette's tragedy, Mason, "grinning hypocrite" and "coward" (40,47), blindly lays the foundation for Antoinette's tragedy by means of an arranged marriage. He supplies the dowry and arranges the marriage: "I want you to be happy, Antoinette, secure, I've tried to arrange.... I have asked some English friends to spend next winter here. You won't be dull" (59). Ironically, just the announcement of this colonial/patriarchal news produces "a feeling of dismay, sadness," and "loss," leading to the second dream which expands the first and foreshadows the colonial and patriarchal oppression and exploitation. The first dream occurs at Coulibri (26-27), and it is repeated two times (59-60, 187-90), each time with "more clarity and detail" (Olaussen 70). It also suggests Antoinette's "fear of sexual violation" (70). The second dream, like the first, precedes Antoinette's tragedy. It prophesies her marriage and so-called madness, links with Mason's manipulating role in marriages, and leaves Antoinette in loneliness. It also foreshadows "Antoinette's departure from the primeval forest of the West Indies to the imprisoning, enclosed garden that is England" (Friedman 125).

Where Mr. Mason's colonizing/patriarchal work ends, his son from a previous marriage, Richard Mason, commences. Richard is at the center of Antoinette's arranged marriage. He panics at Antoinette's reluctance to go through with the marriage (78-79) and gives Antoinette strong "arguments, threats probably," forcing her to keep the arrangement (90-91). Rochester distrusts him (91), and Christophine "is right to blame Richard Mason for his stepsister's affairs" (Le Gallez 143). Christophine echoes Richard's dark side: "Law! The Mason boy fix it, that boy worse than Satan and he burn in hell one of these fine nights" (110). Aunt Cora's argument with Richard Mason also illuminates his corruption: "You are handing over everything the child owns to a perfect stranger" (114).

From Mr. Mason to Richard Mason to Edward Rochester, their economic exploitation of Antoinette fosters her alienation. Rochester's, Antoinette's greatest colonizer, "moral decline of a 'gentle, generous' and 'brave' soul...may be traced to his materialism" (Le Gallez 141). Fragmented and exploited by his wealthy father willing all the family money to the older brother, "Edward is expected to contribute further to that status by taking part in an arranged marriage with a wealthy heiress" in order not to weaken the family status (141). Rochester's hypocritical playacting before the marriage is "a faultless performance," filled with "effort of will," rather than love, leaves Antoinette's hand "cold as ice in the hot sun," and deludes all except the blacks (76-77).

In typical colonial-imposing fashion, Rochester sweeps over Antoinette's fear, concern, and reluctance in preference for his "sad heart," the arrangement, and the "role of rejected suitor jilted by this creole girl" (78-79), because of the strong economic motivation and dictation. The colonizer/Rochester's main objective in a/the relationship with the colony/Antoinette is to 'rape' her and extract all her wealth. Rochester admits his quest for exploitation: "I didn't love her. I was thirsty for her, but that is not love. I felt very little tenderness for her, she was a stranger to me, a stranger who did not think or feel as I did" (93). And "the lack of any 'married woman's property act' ensures that Antoinette's money, on her marriage to Edward, becomes absorbed into his own estate" (Le Gellez 142). Even in the penultimate paragraph of Rochester's narration, as he prepares to return to England, he is obsessed with Antoinette's money: "I'd sell the place for what it would fetch. I had meant to give it back to her. Now— what's the use?" (173). But his letters to his greedy, exploitative father have already provided insights into this economic transaction which leaves Antoinette "a displaced person in her own country" (Howells 111). The letters authenticate that "thirty thousand pounds have been paid to me [Rochester] without question or condition," and that "no provision" has been "made for her" [Antoinette] (70).

Antoinette's money, now in the greedy, grasping hands of Rochester, drives the swindler Daniel Cosway to blackmail for a share of it. Cosway's revengeful exploitation climaxes Rochester's final stranglehold on Antoinette. Daniel Cosway's eurocentric, epistolary method of communication to Rochester parallels Rochester's letters to his father, since both emerge out of a deep fragmented psyche and both seek to extract different measures of recompense. Furthermore, "Rochester, like Cosway, turns hate for his father into hate for Antoinette," claims Angier. She further compares: "Cosway and Rochester share similar characters—even to their ultimate greed, which each gives rein to through a self-righteous desire for vengeance" (162). Cosway's first letter to Rochester alludes to money several times and to the revenge motif: "My momma die when I was quite small and my godmother take care of me. The old mister [Antoinette's father] hand out some money for that though he don't like me. No, that old devil don't like me at all, and when I grow older I see it and I think, Let him wait my day will come" (96). But Antoinette's father and mother are deceased, thereby aborting his plans for revenge. However, Antoinette remains his target, and he, like his namesake, Esau, believes that "Vengeance is mine" (122). Cosway also knows that Mr. Mason has given Antoinette half of his money when he died (97). Cosway wants some of that money, so he mixes facts and fiction to extract money from Rochester, and in the process he further destroys Antoinette's life, love, and marriage. His second letter not only reveals his wickedness, but also his coerciveness: "You want me to come to your house and bawl out your business before everybody? You come to me or I come" (119). Moreover, Amélie confirms Daniel Cosway's imitation of white people and his mysterious life (120–21), while Cosway himself displays his blackmail: "'But if I keep my mouth shut it seems to me you owe me something. What is five hundred pounds to you. To me it's my life.... And if I don't have the money I want you will see what I can do'" (126).

Immediately after reading Cosway's letter, Rochester crushes the flower, foreshadowing his crushing of Antoinette's spirit. He sweats, trembles, sees the day as "far too hot" (99), looks like he has seen a zombie (100), gets lost and becomes afraid (105), and tightens his grip of alienation on Antoinette. He has bound her into economic dependence, rendering her unable to initiate or execute escape. Antoinette explains her economic bondage: "He would never give me any money to go away and he would be furious if I asked him. There would be a scandal if I left him and he hates scandal. Even if I got away (and how?) he would force me back. So would Richard. So would everybody else. Running away from him, from this island, is the lie" (113).

Rochester's actions are controlled by numerous implicating allegations raised in Cosway's letters and conversation. They are against Antoinette's character. But the main explosive bombshell Cosway drops on Rochester is about Antoinette's chastity: "'Your wife know Sandi since long time.... I see them when they think nobody see them. I see her when...You going eh?'" (125). Unable to handle such humiliating news, Rochester darts "to the doorway" (125). But the crafty Cosway shoots his final arrow at the wounded Rochester: "'She start with Sandi. They fool you well about that girl. She look you straight in the eye and talk sweet talk—and it's lies she tell you. Lies. Her mother was so. They say she worse than her mother, and she hardly more than a child. Must be you deaf you don't hear people laughing when you marry her.... You are not the first to kiss her pretty face'" (125–26).

Furiously mad about such an attack on his fragile sexuality, Rochester extracts revenge from Antoinette because "this desire for revenge is still connected to his feelings about his father," and his "anger and hate degenerate into an overt desire to bully, to possess, and to destroy" (Angier 167). He makes love to the rebellious, Amélie, next to his wife's room, and forms another economic exploitative union: "'But she love money like you love money—must be why you come together. Like goes to like'" (149), insinuates Christophine. And Antoinette rebukes Rochester's hypocrisy by comparing him to slave masters: "'You abused the planters and made up stories about them, but you do the same thing. You send the girl away quicker, and with no money or less money, and that's all the difference'" (146).

Despite Fanon's acceptance of Marx's theory of alienation on the basis of economics, his concept of alienation from self also "involves alienation from one's corporeality and personal identity" (Bulhan 188). Fanon distinguishes that "under the German occupation, the French remained men; under the French occupation, the Germans remained men" (*Wretched* 204), but under colonial domination, "a feeling of non existence" emerged (*Black Skin* 139). Hansen explains this concept in the relationship between the colonizer and colonized as "superordination and subordination and superiority and inferiority" (81). Such a concept has become an integral part of the colonial system, and it has dictated the nature of relationships between colonizers and colonized. "Because it is a systematic negation of the other person and a furious determination to deny the other person all attributes of humanity," declares Fanon, "colonialism forces the people it dominates to ask themselves the question constantly: 'In reality, Who am I?'" (*Wretched* 203).

The central question in Antoinette's life is what Coco, her green parrot, asks, "Qui est là? Qui est là?" [Who am I? Who am I?]. Symbolically, Coco answers his own question: "Ché Coco, Ché Coco" (41) before his death by fire, and so Antoinette discovers and defines herself in her leap, not to Rochester, but to Tia, from the burning roof. Desperately trying to escape the negation of her life and to assert her individual identity, Antoinette's efforts at self discovery and definition have encountered colonial and patriarchal domination. "Her fate," postulates Emery, "is shaped by patriarchal colonial authority vested in her husband" (35), and it parallels the fate of the Caribbean, which has been culturally and politically dominated by metropolitan countries.

Antoinette's loss of identity operates in three major ways. In the first case, displacement disrupts her identity. Antoinette loves the Caribbean, especially Coulibri and Dominica, but due to patriarchal and colonial interference from Mason and Rochester, she is uprooted from both places. As discussed earlier, Mason's marriage to Annette is central to the riot at Coulibri, the parallel of Eden (19), and this riot drives the family from their fallen paradise. Antoinette's effort to remain at Coulibri is thwarted by a "jagged stone" from Tia. However, she clings to this place: "As I ran, I thought, I will live with Tia and I will be like her. Not to leave Coulibri. Not to go. Not" (45). Later, in brooding nostalgia, she tells Rochester about the intensity of her love for Dominica and Coulibri: "'I love it [Dominica] more than anywhere in the world. As if it were a person.' 'But you don't know the world,' I teased her. 'No, only here, and Jamaica of course. Coulibri Spanish Town" (89).

Rochester has displaced his wife from Dominica through a reversed but similar middle passage journey of slaves. Antoinette is strong and passionate in the Caribbean landscape which consists of hot sun, green vegetation, and fresh running streams. She is in harmony with this colorful landscape which contains her "tree of life," thereby supplying her with life (19). Antoinette colors her roses in green, blue, and purple, and writes her name in "fire red" (53). But for the wounded and fragmented Rochester, "everything is too much.... Too much blue, too much purple, too much green. The flowers are too red, the mountains are too high, the hills too near. And the woman is a stranger" (70). His failure to control and dominate the landscape renders him powerless: "I wanted to say something reassuring but the scent of the river flowers was overpoweringly strong. I felt giddy" (83), but it also symbolizes his inability to celebrate the colorful and passionate personality and sexuality of his wife. (This point is further discussed under alienation from general other). Threatened and terrified by the landscape, a fearful Rochester "broke a spray off and trampled it into the mud" (99), and his cold and callous way of destroying the landscape symbolizes the way he destroys Antoinette in order to control her. His greedy thirst/lust cannot be satisfied because his colonial perspective associates his hatred to Antoinette and her landscape:

> I hated the mountains and the hills, the rivers and the rain. I hated the sunsets of whatever color, I hated its beauty and its magic and the secret I would never know. I hated its indifference and the cruelty which was part of its loveliness. Above all I hated her. For she belonged to the magic and the loveliness. She had left me thirsty and all my life would be thirst and longing for what I had lost before I found it. (172)

This heavenly place where Antoinette belongs and where she wishes to stay (108), has been made into a hell by Rochester: "But I loved this place and you have made it into a place I hate. I used to think that if everything else went out of my life I would still have this, and now you have spoilt it. It's just somewhere else where I have been unhappy, and the other things are nothing to what has happened here" (147). Angier describes the implication of this destruction. She points out that "in destroying this place for Antoinette, Rochester precipitates her madness because he has destroyed her sense of hope, of belonging, of ownership, autonomy, and ultimately her own sense of personal power" (154). The magnitude of Antoinette's destruction forces her confession to her destroyer: "I hate it now like I hate you and before I die I will show you how much I hate you" (147).

Rochester's deceptive dominance over and destruction of Antoinette (19) have been prophetically illustrated in her first two dreams (26-27, 59-60). His "heavy footsteps" create fear since he hates her (26-27), he soils her "white and beautiful" dress (59), and removes her from the Caribbean to a place where she stumbles on her dress and where "the seconds pass and each one is a thousand years" (60). Stonelike, Rochester completely removes his wife from every trace of the Caribbean landscape. He bluntly denies her request to take the crying boy who "has tried very hard to learn English" (171). And he "can wait—for the day when she is only a memory to be avoided, locked away, and like all memories a legend. Or a lie...." (172).

In the second case, name-changing implicates identity. By the end of Part One, Antoinette writes her name as "Antoinette Mason, née Cosway" (53), but shortly afterwards she adds "Rochester" through marriage. The names Cosway, Mason, and Rochester are all handed down to her from men, colonizers, who have come to the Caribbean to see and conquer. They have been motivated by money and power. Furthermore, they are associated with corruption and madness. Cosway "drank himself to death" and has had many women (29), while Mason has exploited the people he knows so little about that he fails to interpret the surrounding dangers. As Cosway and Mason, Annette represents a haunting past for Antoinette, a past the school girl reminds her of:

> 'Look the crazy girl, you crazy like your mother. Your aunt frightened to have you in the house. She send you for the nuns to lock up. Your mother walk about with no shoes and stockings on her feet, she *sans culottes*. She try to kill her husband and she try to kill you too that day you go to see her. She have eyes like zombie and you have eyes like zombie too.' (49-50)

Later, Daniel Cosway's letters reinforce the theme of inherited madness: "This young Mrs. Cosway is worthless and spoilt.... She shut herself away, laughing and talking to nobody.... The madness gets worse and she has to be shut away for she tried to kill her husband—madness not being all either" (96-97). He also convincingly persuades Rochester that Antoinette "is going the same way as her mother and all knowing it" (98).

Cosway repeatedly refers to Antoinette as Antoinetta, and his influence forces Rochester to conclude that Antoinette will be mad as her mother. Rochester follows Cosway's name-changing and consistently calls her "Bertha," in an effort to erase the identity of Antoinette. Antoinette, of French origin, means "highly praiseworthy," (*Names for Baby* 11), while Bertha "is derived from the Old German meaning 'bright and shining one'" (Nebeker 159). But Rochester's use of "Bertha" conveys a heavy, drugged, and passive personality. He views Antoinette's passionate personality and sexuality as savagery, so he seeks to displace the excited, stimulated, and high powered identity of "Antoinette" with a cold, passive identity of "Bertha." "He calls her Bertha," claims Smilowitz, "in an attempt to disassociate her from her West Indian past, and to establish her rebirth" (102). In this way, argues Emery, "Rochester governors his wife as a master would a slave, and he claims her as a new owner would claim a slave" (46).[6] But Antoinette consistently rejects this new name, claiming that "'Bertha is not my name. You are trying to make me into someone else, calling me by another name. I know that's obeah too'" (147). Furthermore, Rochester dominates her into submission by calling her doll-like names such as "Marionette" in order "to force her to cry and to speak" (154).

In the third case, a divided self promotes an identity crisis. Antoinette, a French creole and West Indian, is warm, sympathetic, and passionate. Her white skin (outer world) isolates her from the blacks who call her "white cockroach" (23), and when she runs to Tia, her black friend and other half, Tia throws a stone at her (45). On the other hand, her passionate feelings (rich inner world) are in tune with the Caribbean environment and the blacks, but alienates her from the whites who call her "white nigger" (102). In the Caribbean, Antoinette's inner and outer worlds are in harmony, but her outer world disagrees with her physical appearance. But in England, her inner and outer worlds are at war, and her outer world agrees with her appearance. She rejects reality, the outer world in England, so her inner dreams flow out to her outer reality. Dreams become reality and reality becomes dreams, so she becomes mad in the eyes of society, but her insanity is perfectly illusive and understandable. Angier postulates that "while Antoinette and Rochester confuse dream and reality, in this collage—and in Antoinette's final dream—dream become reality" (153), and Nebeker adds that Antoinette's madness is "the madness of purpose" (169). Such divided self forces Antoinette to initiate action. She sets the house on fire and leaps to her death and freedom. This action comes just after her final dream on pages 185-88. In this dream and action she consciously affirms her identity by leaping, not to "Bertha! Bertha!" but to Tia, her other half.[7]

The Fanonian formulation of "alienation from the significant other" demonstrates "estrangement from one's family and group" (Bulhan 188). The colonizer's family grows in wholeness, but colonization has fragmented, exploited, and destroyed the colonized family. "Even if the [colonized] family remains relatively intact or little tarnished by this violent social disorder," argues Bulhan, "the attack on the self is merely postponed until one moves away from the intimate circle of the family to the ubiquitous violence of the wider social world." Later, continues Bulhan, the family members will encounter "massive social forces" which "overwhelm their development," and leave them with "inordinate personal conflicts and turmoil" (190-91). These colonial effects are evident in Antoinette's family from the second paragraph of *Wide Sargasso Sea*: "My father, visitors, horses, feeling safe in bed—all belonged to the past" (17). Antoinette's father is deceased, her stepfather is seldom around, so her "mother and Pierre, Christophine, Godfrey, and Sass" are all the people left in her life (22–23). But Annette has failed to save Antoinette from alienation. She "pushed me [Antoinette] away, not roughly but calmly, without a word, as if she had decided once and for all that I was useless to her" (20). So Antoinette quickly "got used to a solitary life" (18), and she "spent most of her time in the kitchen" (20).

This dispossessed, collapsed, and apocalyptic colonial society, in limbo between the emancipation of slavery and the promised English compensation (17), has driven Mr. Luttrell, Annette's neighbor and only friend, to murder his dog and to commit suicide (17), has killed Antoinette's father (28), and has destroyed Annette's security and sanity. Paula Grace Anderson argues that the pressures of poverty, the horse's poisoning, the neighbor's suicide, Pierre's retardation and subsequent death, and Coulibri's destruction, are enough to render Annette insane. And this "final memory" of her mother's "mental decay and sexual abuse" is "prophetically stamped on Antoinette's psyche" (247–48). Moreover, the deaths of her mother and brother and the departures of Mason and Christophine have left Antoinette in complete separation from "the significant other," first at Aunt Cora's house, then at the convent, a place "of death" (56), with "no looking-glass" (54), where she "prayed for a long time to be dead" (57)–her first death.

Marriage to Rochester becomes a reconnection to life as spiritual rebirth is to a sinner.[8] Antoinette's main concern, like a drowning person catching at a straw, is the promise of peace, happiness, and safety (79). Initial happiness follows the marriage, especially with her reconnection with Christophine, her strong, black mother-figure. But, like her raised hope has been shattered by Mr. Mason, her first colonizer, so it is repeated by Rochester, her other colonizer. This is her second death.

Rochester, victim of colonization which has left him a damaged and fragmented individual, can only survive through domination and subsequently destruction of Antoinette—a strong feature of the colonizer-colonized relationship. His displacement in the Caribbean complicates his ruptured personality, leaves him sick "for nearly three weeks out of that time [a month]" (67), and taints his insecure mind to see everything differently from Antoinette (70).[9] Unable to cope with the Caribbean landscape's vibrancy and Antoinette's sexuality, Rochester feels that the place is his enemy (129), so he kills Antoinette by removing her from all the represented significant other, in order to fulfill his Victorian/colonial conception of a submissive wife. Hate, hurt, and revenge prevent him from seeing Antoinette's beauty and virtue; rather, they poison him to murder her, so he covers her as if covering a "dead girl" (138).

Rochester strips Antoinette of all her reconnections and restorations to life. At the crossroad of Antoinette's destiny between life and death and sanity and insanity, when she demonstrates signs bordering on insanity—her fight with Amélie, hair pulling, teeth clenching (100-01)—Rochester fails to save her. Instead, he destroys her by sanctioning Amélie's insubordination and by forcing Christophine to leave. Christophine's second exit from Antoinette signifies her third death, by which time Rochester has metaphorically stripped Antoinette, and only Christophine can rescue her. However, her desperate efforts in the forms of obeah—"love potion" (116-18), advice for Antoinette to leave Rochester (110), and intervention in the marital dual (144-61), fail to save Antoinette from Rochester's domination and damnation. Trapped, helpless, and lonely, Antoinette embraces violence to freedom: "She smashed another bottle against the wall and stood with broken glass in her hand and murder in her eyes" (148). This powerless colonized/woman's resistance to her colonizer/husband is interpreted and branded as madness by Rochester, which is a Prospero-Caliban kind of stereotypical labeling. Césaire explains that "the colonizer in order to ease his conscience, gets into the habit of seeing the other man as an animal, acustoms himself to treating him like an animal, and tends objectively to transform himself into an animal" (20). In reality, it is Rochester, not Antoinette, who is growing crazy and animalistic.[10] Therefore, like the parrot with clipped wings, she becomes a victim. Stripped of all "significant other," Antoinette lacks support and any means of power to escape marital tragedy and to avoid the reversed Middle Passage because her colonizer does not love her. He "was [only] thirsty for her" (93), and he revenges his fragmentation on her (165-66). She has become his slave, his thing, and his "mad girl" (166), as Caliban has become Prospero's "this thing of darkness I acknowledge mine" (Shakespeare 5. 7. 275).

Alienation from the "general other," is illustrated by "the violence and paranoia characterizing the relation between whites and blacks" (Bulhan 188). Summarizing Fanon's theories, Bulhan remarks: "It is particularly when the black person is cut off from his community and thrown into the world that structural, institutional, and personal violence intensifies and psycho-existential crisis unfolds with poignancy" (192). Under colonization, Antoinette and her family experience fluctuating alienation from the wider community—blacks and whites, and through this racially based alienation, Antoinette has been repeatedly denied her other—black consciousness, which can be seen through her relationship with Tia, Christophine, and Sandi. Tia represents her black side, her inner consciousness, and her repressed person. Antoinette and Tia soon become friends: "Tia was my friend and I met her nearly every morning at the turn of the road to the river." They light fires, boil "green bananas," and eat them with their fingers (23). But post-slavery society pressures any interracial relationship.[11] Antoinette and Tia can only meet out of the public's sight, and soon they fulfill societal expectations as they verbalize: "Keep them you cheating nigger," Antoinette tiredly declared. But Tia responds: "Old time white people nothing but white nigger now, and black nigger better than white nigger" (24). Furthermore, the cross-dressing, through an act of thievery on Tia's part, evokes repression and disassociation: "Throw away that thing. Burn it" (25).

In a displacing, departing, and defining scene of riot, Antoinette recognizes that elements of her white self would be destroyed: "The golden ferns and the silver ferns, the orchids, the ginger lilies and the roses, the rocking chairs and the blue sofa, the jasmine and the honeysuckle, and the picture of the Miller's daughter" (44-45). Instead of running towards these and other representations of her white self, Antoinette publicly demonstrates/testifies her alignment with her black consciousness by running to Tia because "she was all that was left of my [Antoinette's] life as it had been. We had eaten the same food, slept side by side, bathed in the same river. As I ran, I thought, I will live with Tia and I will be like her" (45). But both children are unaware of the powerful dictatorship within the colonial society. The convergence of tears and blood and black and white reflect the meeting of the two halves of Antoinette's whole, but she is denied her otherness:

> When I was close I saw the jagged stone in her hand but I did not see her throw it. I did not feel it either, only something wet, running down my face. I looked at her and I saw her face crumple up as she began to cry. We stared at each other, blood on my face, tears on hers. It was as if I saw myself. Like in a looking glass. (45)

Commenting on this point, Emery reinforces that "the doubling of Tia and Antoinette in this confrontation poses them simultaneously as Other and the same," and that "the violent circumstances that divide them also bind them in imagined reflections of one another" (42).[12]

In a circular pattern of highly symbolic events, Antoinette finally discovers and defines herself, thereby releasing her suppressed black half (187-90). This final meeting of Antoinette with her otherness, Tia, depicts both Antoinette and Tia's, white and black's, transcendence of colonial racism. Again, recognizing her white side of "grandfather's clock," "doll's house and the books and picture of the Miller's Daughter" and hearing Rochester's call of "Bertha! Bertha!" (189), Antoinette calls "Tia" and identifies with her black other. This time Tia beckons to her, laughs with her, and asks, "you frightened?" (190). All her life, her black consciousness has been made a prisoner of her white skin. Now, Antoinette realizes that Tia represents that part of life she does not want to part with, but if sanity and status in the colonial convention means continual suppression of this otherness, Antoinette musters courage, in logical sanity, and defies the status quo.

Throughout Antoinette's life she has tried to allow the black part of her life to be fully lived out, but constant colonial and patriarchal suppression has denied her other self. At another level, Antoinette's black consciousness emerges from her daughter–mother relationship with Christophine, her black mother who is there for her. Colonial complications have denied Antoinette and her mother, Annette, the opportunity to share a normal mother–daughter relationship. Colonial society has destroyed Annette physically, socially, mentally, and spiritually, leaving Antoinette a lonely individual with a fragmented past, a fluctuating present, and an uncertain future. From Antoinette's early tragedy, "Christophine stayed with me because she wanted to stay.... I dare say we would have died if she'd turned against us and that would have been a better fate. To die and be forgotten and at peace. Not to know that one is abandoned, lied about, helpless" (21–22).

Christophine provides a friend and playmate for Antoinette (23), she is concerned about Antoinette's training and upbringing (26), she dresses her, curls her hair (28), answers important questions (36), provides security (37), and fights for her. The bond between Antoinette and Christophine provides teaching, strength, and refuge, and this bond threatens the colonizer's security because it provides for Antoinette's holistic development, including her suppressed black half. For this reason, Mason has tried to replace Antoinette's black consciousness with new servants' cooking: "We ate English food now, beef and mutton, pies and puddings" (35), but although she "was glad to be like an English girl," she "missed the taste of Christophine's cooking" (35). However, warns Emery, Antoinette's submission to "the neocolonist Mason's plans" can seriously displace her from the island's people who are primarily black (39).

Similarly, Rochester's security is ruptured by the bond between Antoinette and Christophine, so he destroys it by blaming her for Antoinette's tragedy and by separating them (159–61). Furthermore, Christophine's philosophy and perspective are in direct contrast to those of Rochester. Christophine represents the fulfilling, celebratory, liberating, independent, and feminist side of Antoinette, while Rochester accounts for the opposite of these in Antoinette's life. For example, Christophine claims that whatever she sees exists, and whatever she cannot see does not exist. She transfers this philosophy to her view of England which she claims does not exist. Therefore, Antoinette believes and experiences this. She sees England as an illusion and the Caribbean as reality (110–12). But for Rochester, the Caribbean is unreal and England is real (80-81).    Additionally, Rochester destroys Christophine's efforts to re-lease Antoinette's black self because he cannot understand or share the other side of his wife. He resents Antoinette's communication with Christophine, especially in patois (91), and questions, "Why do you hug and kiss Christo-phine?" because he "wouldn't hug and kiss them [blacks]," he "couldn't" (91).

Perhaps the greatest area of concern for the colonizer/male is Antoinette's sexuality. Mason allows his son, Richard, freedom and flexibility to attend school in Barbados. Richard will later go to England (31-32). There is no worry about the corruption or exploitation of his sexuality, but, at seventeen plus, Antoinette's first teenage love affair with Sandi is swiftly disrupted by Mason's speedy marriage arrangement (58-59). This is another important al-ienation from the general other because Sandi, Daniel Cosway's half brother's (Alexander Cosway) son, is black, even though he is "like a white man, but more handsome than any white man" (125). This black boy, "a projection of that unified self" (Nebeker 142), loves Antoinette, cares for her, shares with her, respects her, and values her as a person. Unlike Rochester, Sandi, An-toinette's cousin, does not exploit or oppress her. Rather, he has rescued and protected Antoinette from her enemies, he has secured her dropped book and returned it to her, and he has pursued the enemy to ensure Antoinette's fu-ture security (50-51). Sandi has taught her to aim well (88), but Antoinette has had to deny any connection with Sandi because of race. Anderson points out that "Rhys exposes the integrated racism and neocolonialistic class preju-dice that dictate that Antoinette cannot marry her psychic bridegroom, her distant cousin, protector, mentor, the mulatto, Sandi" (249). Early in the novel, Antoinette reports this denial of her first other black half: "Once I would have said 'my cousin Sandi' but Mr. Mason's lectures had made me shy about my colored relatives" (50). And it is this "longing for, the search for, the finding of the integrated SELF which is the beginning and the end of 'being,' and the whole purpose behind the act of love" (142), argues Nebeker.[13]

Rochester, coming from a cold and corrupted culture, fails to love An-toinette and cannot understand and appreciate her love. Staley enlightens that "Edward comes from another world and cannot fathom the life of the pas-sions; everything in the natural surroundings which epitomizes sensuous beauty tells him that this is Antoinette's world, and this is why he fears it from the beginning" (114-15). He wants an object and a passive partner. His frag-ile/wounded sexuality and ego are at the center of his final domination and destruction of Antoinette. Before the marriage, Antoinette's refusal to marry him causes his egocentricity to surface: "He [Richard] went out meekly and while I dressed I thought that this would indeed make a fool of me. I did not relish going back to England in the role of rejected suitor jilted by this creole girl" (78). Later, the major worrying concern of Daniel Cosway's letters (95–99 and 118–19) and conversation (122–26) is not the alleged madness of the family, but the colonizer's/Rochester's sexual defeat from the colonized/Sandi (125–26).[14] He resolves not to leave Antoinette for anyone else, and as he is challenged to love her once more, he remembers Cosway's words: "*(Give my sister your wife a kiss from me)*" (158). Furthermore, Christophine's suggestion of a divorce strikes at his fragile sexuality: "'She marry with someone else. She forget about you and live happy.' A pang of rage and jealousy shot through me [Rochester]. Oh no, she won't forget. I laughed" (159). In fact, after this discovery about Antoinette's love affair with Sandi, Rochester acts like a crazy man. He makes love with Amélie, gets rid of Christophine, and departs for England, with his conquered slave and secret. Moreover, Rochester is too ashamed to narrate the episode of Antoinette's love affair with Sandi. It is not that he is unaware of the continued relationship, for "he had found out that Sandi had been to the house and that I [Antoinette] went to see him [Sandi]" (186). But Antoinette, Rochester's supposedly mad wife, logically and clearly illuminates the readers, in part three, that "Sandi often came to see me when that man was away and when I went out driving I would meet him.... The servants knew, but none of them told" (185).

Cultural alienation involves "estrangement from one's language and history," and it exemplifies "the imposition of a European language on blacks in the diaspora" (Bulhan 188–89). According to Fanon, "to speak a language is to take on a world, a culture" (*Black Skin* 38). Bulhan elaborates Fanon's theory by pointing out that "the fact of having to speak nothing but the other's language when this other was the conqueror, ruler, and oppressor was at once an affirmation of him, his worldview, and his values; a concession to his framework; and an estrangement from one's history, values, and outlook." Bulhan further points out:

> The imposition of European culture and language on blacks in the diaspora was realized through massive violence, forcing the history, culture, and genealogy of blacks into oblivion. Culture always has had an intimate, dialectical link with the existence.... Cultural deracination of blacks was but the intellectual and emotional counterpart of economic enslavement. The Middle Passage uprooted *bodies*, transporting them to alien lands. Cultural deracination dislocated *psyche*, imposing an alien world view. (189)

Although a white creole, Antoinette has had more exposure to the black Caribbean language and culture. Alienated quite early from the whites, Antoinette's friend is Tia, her lover is Sandi, her mother-figure is Christophine, and her servants include Amélie, Bertrand, Baptiste, Hilda, and Rose. This close, black community acculturates her, but her colonizers, Mason and Rochester, deny her a rich black culture—the tree of life—and impose white European culture on her. Caught between two vastly different cultures, Antoinette is torn apart, and she questions her "nationality, birth, and personal identity," and feels lost (Emery 35). Antoinette's central question alludes to her crucial cultural dilemma: "So between you both I often wonder who I am and where is my country and where do I belong and why was I even born at all" (102). She is bifurcated by the two cultures Rochester and Christophine represent (Emery 35), and she is also dominated by the dominant culture, the colonizer's culture.

I have already discussed important aspects of cultural alienation—food, landscape—therefore, my focus here will be on language and dress. According to Edward Said, "language itself is a highly organized and encoded system, which employs many devices to express, indicate, exchange messages and information" (qtd. in Gikandi, *Reading Chinua Achebe* 24). Susan Beckman adds that "language is everything you do" (66). Therefore, language is culture, and its role in colonial alienation is nicely illustrated by Richard Onwuanibe. Using Fanon's *Black Skin White Masks* as a theoretical base, Onwuanibe points out that "one of the major aspects of alienation is cultural imposition in the form of language" which "incarnates and expresses the culture of a people." As a result of this any "deprivation of language amounts to a deprivation of a person's humanity" which causes the objectification of that person (42). In Prospero-like manner, Rochester seeks to impose language on Antoinette.

Antoinette's language reflects richness in description, emotion, and sensory details. The following passage from Part Two is a good example of the above point:

> I can remember every second of that morning, if I shut my eyes I can see the deep blue colour of the sky and the mango leaves, the pink and red hibiscus, the yellow handkerchief she wore around her head, tied in the Martinique fashion with the sharp points in front, but now I see everything still, fixed forever like the colours in a stained-glass window. Only the clouds move. It was wrapped in a leaf, what she had given me, and I felt it cool and smooth against my skin. (118)

But Rochester's language lacks sensory detail and emotional and descriptive richness. His language is bare. The beginning of Part Two records this plain Eurocentric language: "So it was all over, the advance and retreat, the doubts and hesitations. Everything finished, for better or for worse" (65). He loves numbers and figures: "2,000 feet," "the thirty thousand pounds have been paid to me" (70), "I was down with fever for two weeks" (76). His "narrative begins in a jaded voice and uses the vocabulary of war," cites Angier, whereas Antoinette's conversation with Sister Marie Augustine, at the end of Part One, is "both evocative and sympathetic" (158). Furthermore, his longer narrative reveals the complex and controlling aspects of his character (Angier 170), and he lacks the language to describe his violent love-making with Antoinette (Louis 59). Nevertheless, by the end of Antoinette's brief narrative in Part Two, Rochester's language begins to resemble Antoinette's:

> I sat on the Veranda with my back to the sea and it was as if I had done it all my life. I could not imagine different weather or a different sky. I knew the shape of the mountains as well as the shape of the two brown jugs filled with white sweet-scented flowers on the wooden table. I knew that the girl would be wearing a white dress. Brown and white she would be, her curls, her white girl's hair she called it, half covered with a red handkerchief, her feet bare. There would be the sky and the mountains, the flowers and the girl and the feeling that all this was a nightmare, the faint consoling hope that I might wake up. (119)

Angier indicates that "for the first time," Rochester's language is "remarkably similar to Antoinette's, both in terms of the kind of detail—the sensual, visual aspects of the flowers, the colours of the girl—and in terms of its wistfulness" (155). But Rochester, steeped in colonial thinking, cannot afford to be sucked into Antoinette's/the colonized's language. This would minimize his status. Thus, Rochester dominates Antoinette through linguistic and cultural anesthesia, in order to recover his Prospero-like language.

Born to Annette, a Creole West Indian, and bred on "the music of the native dreams," "Godfrey's...grumblings, and Christophine's...music" (Nebeker 140), Antoinette's whole cultural orientation is aligned with black Caribbean culture. In fact her main language influence emerges from Christophine whose language reflects rhythmic, musical, and revolutionary strength of Caribbean culture: "'Taste my bull's blood, master'.... 'Not horse piss like the English madams drink,'...'I know them. Drink drink their yellow horse piss, talk, talk their lying talk'" (85). While Christophine's language flows from a rich historical, multicultural tradition and it sounds exquisitely wonderful in Antoinette's ears, it offends Rochester's British sensibility because to him "it is horrible" (85). Later, Rochester demonstrates his intolerance of Antoinette's communication with Christophine in patois (91), and Rochester's rejection of the natives' language documents the colonizers' (Dutch, French, Spanish and British) rejection of Caribbean's talki talki, patois, paimento, and creolese.[15] Moreover, he becomes afraid of what he perceives to be Antoinette's imitation of a "negro's voice, singing and insolent" (129), and from his dominant position he rejects Antoinette's language and culture as madness and Christophine's culture as sinful and illegal obeah.[16] Therefore, "Antoinette is, like her island, 'colonized,' her independence and autonomy subsumed to British culture and to British law" (Angier 193). And

Christophine's obeah, like the indigenous culture, has been silenced after being branded a paganistic culture.

Someone has said that a dress on a woman is like an address on a letter indicating its intended destination. In the multicultural, multiracial, and colorful Caribbean, dress becomes one of the means for Antoinette to recognize her mother in the mental asylum (48), while in England, Antoinette believes if she had been wearing her red dress, Richard would have recognized her (184). Dressing also indicates important cultural practices and spiritual and psychological conditions of one's personality. Totally ignorant of the natives' culture and fully unprepared to learn, Rochester makes a series of blunders in his colonial stereotypical condemnation of Christophine. Even after he learns from Antoinette that "'when they [natives] don't hold their dress up it's for respect'.... 'Or for feast days or going to Mass,'" Rochester completely ignores the significance of the custom: "'Whatever the reason it is not a clean habit'" (85).

Antoinette's assimilation of the culture, Tia's culture, through the wearing of Tia's dress encounters sharp disapproval from her mother who is now in the presence of Mason. Emery points out that "in the black child's dress, Antoinette arrives home to meet a visitor from England, Mr. Mason, who eventually marries her mother and takes over their neglected estate. She has become Tia's double, by a forced exchange, and in that costume meets the man who will forcefully exchange her in marriage to another white Englishman." The old muslin dress being forced on her, is torn, depicting "Antoinette's previous identity no longer fits" (Emory 39). And in a week from Mason's visit, Antoinette and her mother have new dresses (27). However, Antoinette, like the colonized, has been stripped of her culture, and her nakedness earns repeated dressing advice. "'Get up and dress yourself'" (37), Annette tells her, just before Coulibri's fire. At the collapse of her marriage, stripped of a pseudo-culture from Rochester and Mason, Christophine invites Antoinette towards decolonization: "Get up, girl, and dress yourself. Woman must have spunks to live in this wicked world" (101). Discover and define your cultural identity through independence in order to survive colonial exploitation and displacement, alludes Christophine. But Antoinette, like the colony, has little or no choice in her dressing. For her dressing is controlled during childhood by Annette, adolescence by Mason, and adulthood by Rochester.

For the British, things, including dresses, must be black or white. While Antoinette wears a white bridal dress, the women (cousin Julia, cousin Ada, Aunt Lina) "in another room" are "dressed in black.... Thin or fat they all looked alike" (77). The lack of variety or coloration is what Rochester dresses Antoinette with: "She was wearing the white dress I had admired" (127), and two pages later he places the yellow shawl [close to white] around her shoulders (129). But variety and color are essential to Caribbean culture, the tree of life, from which Antoinette feeds. Therefore, stripped once in her own country and now in England, the "cardboard world" where there is no mirror, her red dress becomes culturally significant, since it links her with the Caribbean landscape (fire, sun, flowers)), the meaning of time, passionate memory with Sandi (183), and recognition (184). In her final effort to discover and define her cultural identity, she recreates the Caribbean culture, and fire and the red dress become significant symbols in this recreation: "I let the dress fall on the floor, and looked from the fire to the dress and from the dress to the fire" (186). In this symbolic connection, fire becomes the method by which she defines her cultural identity, while the red dress becomes the message of her Caribbean cultural definition. Angier concludes that Antoinette's "obsession with the red dress" becomes "a symbol of another reality, another time, and another place" (153).

# Notes

1.  Helen Tiffin's point is useful at this juncture. She indicates that "in the marriage between Antoinette Cosway and Edward Rochester, the imperial/colonial relation is clear. . . . Antoinette is literally Rochester's prisoner in England. She is friendless, has lost her own name, and is regarded as a wild animal who must be restrained by her captors" (338).

2.  In the introduction I pointed out that economics has been the major motivation behind colonization, giving rise to psychological dynamics in the relationship between the colonizer and the colonized. O. Mannoni and Albert Memmi are at the center of the exploration of this psychoanalytical relationship. However, I need to point out that Fanon's concept of the psychology of the relationship differs from O. Mannoni.

3.  Memmi's statement reinforces the point: "Colonization is, above all, economic and political exploitation" (149).

4.  A short version of this section has been presented in chapter 5, section 1. The expansion of this version is necessary for contextualization understanding.

5.  The exslaves also allude that Mr. Cosway's, Antoinette's father, degenerated economy, resulting from emancipation, has caused his death (28).

6.  Nebeker adds that Rochester's renaming of Antoinette has stripped her "individual essence, domesticating and gaining control by denying her alien heritage. More importantly however, he unconsciously reveals his fear of all she represents to her" (159).

7.  Several interpretations have emerged about the ending of the novel. Emery has no doubt that Antoinette commits suicide: "Her only act, the torching of Thornfield Hall, enables a morally ambiguous resolution, through suicide" (36). Carole Angier believes that Antoinette's action "sets her free," and it represents "her own Phoenix-like fantasy of recapitulation and regeneration" (153), while Paula Grace Anderson interprets existentially, "not as a desperate abdication from life but rather as a celebration of that life which she once knew in the Caribbean, in all its intensity, whether negative or positive" (245). But Nebeker interprets that, in her phantasy, Antoinette leaps into the "'pool at Coulibri' where Tia, her other half, still laughs and beckons"(170).

8.  The reference comes from Christ's statement to Nicodemus: "Except a man be born again, he cannot see the kingdom of God" (John 3:3). Matthew Henry explains that

the new birth means beginning from the "foundation," having new "principles, new affections, new aims," and receiving "divine and heavenly life" (315). Merrill Tenney adds that the "natural man" is "inherently incapable of apprehending it [the new birth], just as a blind man cannot enjoy a sunset. . . . Just as an infant, by the very occurrence of his birth, is fitted for a new life in a strange realm, so men must experience spiritual rebirth preparatory to their entrance into the kingdom of God" (86).

9.  See text, page 70, for an example of Rochester's negative perception of the Caribbean landscape.

10. See epigram. Erika Smilowitz also points out that Conrad's *Heart of Darkness* and Forster's *A Passage to India* illustrate this animalistic transformation of the colonizers (100).

11. James Louis reinforces that "social pressures also undermine Antoinette's friendship with Tia" (53).

12. See Wilson Harris's *The Womb of Space* for "cross–cultural connections" between Antoinette and the Amerindians and between Christophine's obeah and Antoinette's Catholicism (50). See also Margaret Paul Joseph's "Bottomless Inquisition," especially pages 36–38.

13. See also James Louis who claims that "the tragedy is that race and social constraints have prevented the natural relationship between Antoinette and the tall genteel mulatto from culminating in marriage" (53).

14. Thomas F. Staley links Rochester's response of sexual fear to "Gabriel Conroy's reaction to his wife's, Gretta's, recollection of her dead lover Michael Fury in Joyce's 'The Dead', not in the mode of revelation, but rather in the way in which the two men's egos operate." He further points out that Edward's response springs from loneliness because he is "wounded and outraged. Like Gabriel, Edward's inflated pride and imperious personality entrap his feelings exclusively in the self" (110).

15. Deena discusses the political implications of language.

16. I say sinful and illegal because the colonizer makes and enforces the laws and judges the colonized by the laws. Therefore, while his type of obeah is perfect, that of the natives is seen as hideous. The white magic of Prospero is viewed as intellectual, artistic, and imaginative, but Caliban's black magic is seen as dark, demonic, and destructive, and that is why Ariel is preferred to Caliban.

# Conclusion

My conclusion is unorthodox. I have decided to highlight four important catalysts in Caribbean literature, culture, religion, sports, and education—Phillip Mohabir, Gay Wilentz, Oscar Ronald Dathorne, and Winston McGowan—and mention a few journals and conferences that explore Caribbean studies. Not much is publicized on these four multicultural and postcolonial figures, yet they have played significant roles in advancing Caribbean Studies as central to multicultural and postcolonial discourses.

## Philip Mohabir: Interracial, Intercultural, and International Reconciler and Bridge-builder

The shattering effects of colonialism have posed new and complicating problems for the 21$^{st}$ century on both a national and international scale. War, genocide, poverty, and exploitation necessitate proclamations of love, forgiveness, and hope for global and cultural healing and health. Contemporary methodologies of these proclamations by people of respect and repute offer the potential for reconciliation and restoration. Philip Mohabir has joined a select group of humanitarians like Mahatma Gandhi, Mother Theresa, Martin Luther King, Jr., and others. While his influences of peace, love, healing, and international understanding have had profound effects on colonial and postcolonial societies, he remains absent in the USA from many discussions on the affects of colonialism as well as forums seeking solutions to plights of the postmodern world. His death in November 2004 would have silenced this legendary man if not for the persistence of a voice that taught faith, charity, and compassion. Though Philip can no longer relate to us the moments that defined the man he became and the legacy he would leave; his wife, children, siblings, friends, and disciples have a lifetime of memories that will allow us to gain a better understanding of both Philip and the message of peace he taught in the midst of racial and religious conflicts. Philip traveled extensively over the world, spending most of his time in England and Guyana. Much of his untold story waits there in the form of guarded oral tradition.

Philip's first breath was of colonial oppression on a sugar plantation in British Guiana. Born to indentured servants brought from India to replace the emancipated slaves of the Caribbean, he witnessed early in life the horrors of colonialism he would later speak against. Arriving in England as a teenager in 1956, Philip was shocked at London's spiritual wilderness and racial turbulence. By a miracle of grace, he responded not with bitterness to religious, cultural, and racial discrimination, but with determination to build bridges between black and white. From London to Sweden, to the West Indies, Africa, Asia, USA, and once more to London, Philip impacted the culture, worldview, and vision of masses of peoples—founding the networks of (ICLC)[1], (ACEA)[2], (CN)[3], (FGF)[4], and several other international, intercultural, and interracial organizations.

During the 1960s as British Guiana pressed her case for independence, major racial conflicts—colonial destabilizing strategy—riled the country as the people of Indian and African decent fought a brutal racial battle, resulting in the deaths of thousands of people. Though interracial and intercultural divides were hauntingly deep, he returned to his homeland with Muriel, his Jamaican wife of African descent, and his children and became a major voice of reconciliation and toleration in British Guiana for the next two decades.

The quest to better understand Philip is an international project that will benefit the pursuit of international and intercultural understanding. On a global scale, it will benefit the world by showing peaceful solutions—in the realms of Mahatma Gandhi, Mother Theresa, and Martin Luther King, Jr.—to recent problems caused by international, interracial, and intercultural misunderstanding. Philip's influence, life, message, and work have been "like a bridge over troubled waters" reconciling these divides. By better understanding the voice that shattered the darkness of racial inequality and violence in Guyana and England, we are able to teach, read, and follow the paths left by this reconciler and bridge-builder, whose life has left a legacy of limitless love.

Phillip has left behind his widow, Muriel, their six children, and several grandchildren and a lasting impact on the global community in the areas of racial and religious reconciliation, especially with his emphasis on the following principles as solutions: Commitment to Relationship, Intentionality, Sincerity, Sensitivity, Interdependence, Sacrifice, Empowerment, and Call. He was "small in stature, but he cast a large shadow," (Dave Tom), and his shadow gave voice and power to the poor, exploited, marginalized, and oppressed across the world, especially from the Caribbean. He has also written several books including: *Building Bridges, Pioneers or Settlers, Worlds Within Reach: Cross-cultural Witness,* and *Hands of Jesus,* has given thousands of speeches all over the world, and written hundreds of letters. I was privileged to be in his presence on several occasions, to listen to many of his messages, to read his books, to teach in some of his leadership conferences, and to gain insights from his experience and wisdom. He has done much for the restoration of humanity globally, but especially in the Caribbean.

## Gay Wilentz: Scholar, Pioneer, Teacher

I have been blessed to know and work with Professor Gay Wilentz for 12 years, as the founder and Co-coordinator of the Graduate Multicultural Literature Program and the Director of the Ethnic Studies Program at East Carolina University. Additionally, I have worked very closely with her on an exchange program with the University of Belize, and most importantly, I was her colleague, and friend. Though not from the Caribbean, she became a West Indian—especially a Belizean.

Professor Wilentz was a real pioneer in her research, service, and teaching. Her books have been groundbreaking, and her recent work with Belizean writers has not only realized several books, but has also changed the landscape of academics in that country. Professor Wilentz's chapter, "Judaizing the Secret Practices: Religion and Crypto-Jews in Mexico through Kathleen Achalá's *Spirits of the Ordinary,*" in *From Around the Globe: Secular Authors and Biblical Perspectives,* is another pioneering research territory that she began to uncover just before her early death, and it promised cutting-edge scholarship for the future.

As a person Professor Wilentz was amiable, honest, kind, determined, responsible, warm, daring, and hardworking. She pursued excellence in all areas, and was strongly motivated in her research, service, and teaching. Her art was sacred and diverse. Her compassion, perception, and diligence aided her high level of achievement and success.

Professor Wilentz's administrative ability and excellent performance, interpersonal skills, and leadership ability have been demonstrated consistently in and outside the classroom. She was a very resourceful and creative leader, and her maturity further enhanced the quality of her personality and profession. Students respected and responded to her leadership.

A very matured, centered, and clearly focused individual, Professor Wilentz made us proud at East Carolina University, contributing not only through scholarship and critical presence, but also through her willingness to undertake extra-curricular service and her pioneering spirit to aid development. Her initiative and creativity added depth to her contribution. She was the kind of scholar that would enhance any organization's reputation.

On the morning I received the news of her death, I was shocked and saddened of the passing away of my friend, our friend, a friend of the Caribbean. I closed my office door and wept. "Can the Subaltern Speak" when "A Woman of the People," has gone to greater explorations? I honored her in humble silence like that of the "oum," "oumm" from the sacred caves. When I thought I could speak, I went to Professor Rick Taylor's office. We hugged and wept. Unable to speak, we squeezed each other, and said much more than words. With our candidate on campus that day and my classes to teach, I prayed for strength to get through a very long day, one I will never forget.

Yesterday "Death, that strange being with the huge square toes who lived way in the West," came to my friend (Hurston 129), and she went quietly, I thought the day after her death. I then repeated the lines from Dylan Thomas's poem, "Do Not Go Gentle into that Good Night":

And you, my [friend], there on the [happy] height,
[Have blessed us all with smiles so bright].
[I pleaded with you not to go gentle into that good night].
But to rage against the dying of the light. (Dylan Thomas)

You were too brilliant and too young to die, but you had to go.

I was blessed to know her and to work with her. We had lots of frolic and fulfillment as we worked very closely with our students and the exchange programs with Belize and Ghana, and as we talked and dreamed about extending our work in Guyana. They say we grow old when regrets replace dreams. Gay never grew old.

Summer 2007 was special! We had one house in Belize, one door key, one speech, one TV, and in many ways one heart. I learned to die to myself so that Gay would live, and in dying I resurrected to newness of life, love, and laughter. I love sports and news; Gay loved movies. The NBA finals were on, but we watched movies. We wept, we embraced, and we communicated in a new language. We watched *Hotel Rawanda*, again. Gay wept openly and continuously; I did silently and continuously. We knew our hearts beat for the same/similar causes. We hugged and silently said a million words. Then came the tablet and writing (Gay's ALS deteriorated rapidly destroying her ability to speak). I responded by writing, until Gay reminded me that I could speak.

It was during that time, when things were happening too quickly, and when I was discovering the depth of Gay's illness, and when I wanted to run away and not be the one to see my friend struggle painfully, and when I had to be honest with our students, and yet protect them, that I had a long and deep look into a great mind and soul. I saw more clearly how sacred and diverse was Gay's art of research and teaching. How committed she was to her students and the people of Belize, and how much more she had to work to prepare for her class. And couple of times, she expressed her tiredness of adjusting to her illness, but quickly recovered reminding me how much her students and the Belizeans loved her. In a way, Gay exceeded the Scottish doctor and missionary David Livingstone, whose heart is buried in Africa, but his body is buried in England. She gave both her heart and body to Belize and the Caribbean.

It was painful for me to watch her struggle daily, but it was joyful for me to serve her, and for me to learn from her. Though afflicted with pain temporarily, she celebrated with a view for eternity. Gay's resilience and optimism made me believe she was going to fulfill another dream of going with me to Guyana and realize the online program for the students in Guyana and Belize.

Gay has carved a unique voice of national and international recognition in a very short time. Her initiative and creativity have also added several new pathways to international, multicultural, and interdisciplinary programs at East Carolina University; and her solid and cutting-edge scholarship and the unique graduate multicultural literature program were key factors in attracting me to East Carolina University in the face of other more lucrative job offers.

The first time Gay and I spoke on the phone in February 1994, we talked about her favorite writer, Wilson Harris, about Guyana, and about the Caribbean. Her voice was warm, welcoming, and inclusive. I was ready to come to ECU, my new home, where I just discovered one of my new Caribbean sisters.

Gay ran her race quickly, and finished her course brilliantly. Her life and works gave voice and power to the poor, exploited, marginalized, and oppressed across the world, especially women and Belizeans. Her works include: *Healing Narratives: Women Writers Curing Dis-Ease, Emerging Perspectives on Ama Ata Aidoo, Memories Dreams and Nightmares: A Short Story Anthology by Belizean Women Writers*, and *White Patron and Black Artist: The correspondence of Fannie Hurst and Zora Neale Hurston*.

## Oscar Ronald Dathorne—Poet, Novelist, Critic, Scholar, and Educator: Pioneer of Multicultural and Postcolonial Explorations of Black Diasporic Studies

The Academy (Scholarship) is obsolete without involvement in the community. O R Dathorne (1934-2007), a late contemporary of Franz Fanon, Aime Cesaire, Wilson Harris, Richard Wright, Walter Rodney, Derek Walcott, and others, through the academy, has left the global community a legacy of his pioneering scholarship of Black Diasporic Studies through a multicultural and postcolonial lens. While Ronald Dathorne's work as a pioneer of multicultural and postcolonial explorations of Black Diasporic Studies has had profound effects on colonial and postcolonial societies—namely England, Africa, and the Caribbean, he remains partially absent in the USA from many discussions on the affects of colonialism and the importance of Black Diasporic Studies in multicultural America. His unexpected death in December 2007 was a shock to all, but especially to me, since I was scheduled to spend several sessions with him and his works before writing a book on his pioneering contribution to Black Diasporic Studies. Though Ronald can no longer relate to us the moments that defined the man he became and the legacy he would leave the academy and community, his wife, children, siblings, friends, and works have a lifetime of memories that will allow us to gain a better understanding of the thought, writing, and teaching of Ronald and his global perspective of the interconnection and interdependence of the growing Black Diaspora.

Ronald has traveled extensively over the world, spending most of his time in Guyana, England, Africa, and the United States of America. Born and raised in the complex and diverse British Guiana, Ronald was quickly introduced to the social conflicts of race, class, and status that resulted from colonialism, and because he did not fit into any one group, he became a questioner and a challenger, a social critic with little patience for the hypocrisy and unfairness he saw around him. He was unhappy at the prestigious colonial, male high school, Queen's College, because of racial prejudice.

After graduation from high school in 1953, Ronald went to England to continue his education. He worked for two years as a clerk in the office of the London County Council, while studying the advanced Latin he needed to be accepted into a British university. Ronald received his bachelor's degree in English from the University of Sheffield in 1958, and studied education at the University of London for a year (Certificate of Education, 1959) before returning to Sheffield to pursue his master's (1960) and doctoral (1966) degrees, and going to the University of London for his Diploma in Education,

English as a Foreign Language (1967). Later, in the USA, at the University of Miami, he completed his MBA, Business Administration, and MPA, Public Affairs (1983). Ronald was always reading, researching, writing, and exploring, even in his last weeks.

The wealth of knowledge and experience Ronald has gained, from both the colonial and colonized and black and white worlds, has made his life and works invaluable cutting-edge 21$^{st}$ century scholarship for both the global academy and community, especially for a global community that is lacerated by racial, ethnic, and religious conflicts. His service included: Ahmadu Bello University, Zaria, Nigeria, assistant professor, 1959-63; University of Ibadan, Nigeria, associate professor, 1963-6; United Nations Educational, Scientific and Cultural Organization Milton Magai Training College, 1967-70; University of Sierra Leone at Njala, English Department, Chair and Professor of English Literature and Black Literature, 1967-70; Yale University, Visiting Professor, 1970; Howard University, Department of African Studies, Professor, 1970-1; University of Wisconsin, Department of Afro-American Studies, Professor, 1970-1; Ohio State University, Department of English, Professor, Department of Black Studies, Professor and Co-director, 1971-7; University of Miami, Caribbean, African, and African American Studies Program, Director and Professor of English, 1977-87; University of Kentucky, English Department, Professor, 1987–2007. Additionally, he is/was the Founder and President of the Association of Caribbean Studies (1979-2007) and the Founder and Editor of the *Journal of Caribbean Studies*, (1979-2007).

Much of Ronald's untold story waits in the form of guarded oral tradition, correspondences—especially with other writers and critics, authored works, and read and taught works—especially hand written notes on the pages. The quest then to better understand and articulate Ronald Dathorne's thought and work as a pioneer of multicultural and postcolonial explorations of Black Diasporic Studies is an international, intercultural, and interdisciplinary project that will benefit the world, especially the Caribbean. Conference discussions, scholarly publications, and classroom teachings should examine and explore this fascinating interconnection, which will benefit the world by presenting engaging paradigm shifts in addressing conflicts of race, class, ethnicity, and religion.

Ronald's life and works, especially his almost three decades of dedicated service to the Association of Caribbean Studies and the *Journal of Caribbean Studies*, have shaped and impacted the world, especially the Caribbean, in an unprecedented manner. His works include critical works: *The Black Mind: A History of African Literature, African Literature in the Twentieth Century, Dark Ancestor: The Literature of the Black Man in the Caribbean, In Europe's Image: The Need for American Multiculturalism, Imagining the World: Mythical Belief Versus*

*Reality in Global Encounters, Asian Voyages: Two Thousand Years of Constructing the Other, Worlds Apart: Race in the Modern Period,* novels: *Dumplings in the Soup, The Scholar-Man, Dele's Child,* and poetry: *Songs for a New World.*

He was a true Caribbean man, reflecting the rich racial and cultural hybridity, and he added more to his family with his German wife, Hielde. His quest for intellectual discussion was what drew us together through scholarship, conferences, phone conversations, and reading each other's works. Wherever Ronald went, his calypso music went, and he could spend hours listening to calypso. Additionally, I was amazed at the volume and richness of his library. An entire basement of very expensive books on a wide variety of subjects have been donated to the University of Guyana, and I have managed to get the University of Guyana to honor his legacy by storing his works in a section to be named "Ronald Dathorne Memorial Library."

## Winston McGowan

Winston Franklin McGowan was born in Georgetown in the early nineteen forties in what was then British Guiana to parents of Allison Ewart McGowan & Clarice Florinda McGowan. He received his primary education at the Sacred Heart Roman Catholic School and his secondary education from Queen's College. After graduating from high school, Winston taught for two years at a secondary school before proceeding to the University of the West Indies in Jamaica where he graduated with a Bachelor's of Arts Special Honors Degree in History. Professor Winston McGowan holds a PhD in West African History from the University of London, England. He has been a lecturer in the Department of History at the University of Guyana since October 1970, promoted to Senior Lecturer in 1980 and to Professor in 2000. He served as Head of Department of History from 1986 to 1996, Assistant Dean, Faculty of Arts, 1975 to 1976, and Chair of the Board for Graduate Studies, 1994 to 1996. Currently, he is the second Walter Rodney Chair in History since 2002, and in these capacities he impacted the academic world, especially Guyana and the rest of the Caribbean.

Winston became a committed Christian at the age of 18 just after leaving high school in 1960. Since his commitment to Christ, he has severed the Body of Christ in several capacities. He has been active in the work of Inter-School, Inter-Varsity Christian Fellowship as a club sponsor, President of Inter-Varsity Christian Fellowship group at the University of the West Indies in Jamaica, and a member of the Guyana National Board. In fact, he is a pioneer of Inter-School, Inter-Varsity Christian Fellowship in the Caribbean. Winston has also been very active in the Full Gospel Fellowship in Guyana as a minister, pastor, trustee, and national leader. That's where I first met him in 1976, and I was utterly amazed at his brilliance and humility.

Professor McGowan is also very involved in various Body of Christ ministries in Guyana. He is a prominent member of the Georgetown Ministers Fellowship, mentoring many spiritual leaders, a member of the National Committee of Teen Challenge in Guyana, which is a ministry to rehabilitate drug addicts, and the National Chairman of Intercessors for Guyana, which is a united inter-church prayer movement for Guyana. Stretched and pressed in these commitments, he serves at a distinctive level, and his family has enhanced his authenticity with their exemplary lives.

Perhaps much of Winston's impact is due to his wife, Maureen, of over three decades. She has humbly sacrificed the public for the private, especially in shaping her children and now others. All three of their children have graduated from college. David, the eldest, is a Medical doctor who resides in Jamaica. Christine, the only daughter, is a Lawyer and she and her husband reside in Guyana. Mark, the youngest, is an aspiring journalist and recent graduate of the University of Guyana, and he also resides in Guyana.

What cannot be measured and described by words or appreciation, but only eternity will reveal, is the quality of Dr. McGowan's life, service, relationship, and leadership, and the impact he has had on many areas of Guyana, the Caribbean, and the world. The many social, moral, and spiritual catalysts he has influenced across the world, and how in the midst of economic difficulties in Guyana and the lure of attractive opportunities abroad, he has been firm and constant in his conviction about the potential and global role of Guyana.

Winston has been honored at several forums for a life of excellent and effective service with the global diasporas in education, teaching and preaching, mentoring, sports, and leadership. He can be described as "a man of the people" and for the people as he served them and us with integrity, grace, faithfulness, loyalty, and godliness. He was honored by the government of Guyana in 2002 for his work as an educator and sports commentator with the conferral of a national award, the Arrow of Achievement (A.A.)

Winston remains a solid voice of the Caribbean, and his life and works continue to shape the region, especially Guyana, in an invaluable manner. His publications include 7 books/booklets including, *Themes in African-Guyanese History* (1998) and *Walter Rodney The Historian* (2006), and several scholarly articles including, "The Origins of Slave Rebellions in the Middle Passage," and "African Resistance to the Atlantic Slave Trade in West Africa." His main specialties are African and Guyanese history, the history of slavery in the Americas and the history of revolutionary change. He has also written extensively on cricket. My family and I have been blessed, encouraged, motivated, and impacted by Dr. Winston McGowan and his family.

## Journals and Conferences

Journals include *Callaloo*, *African American Review*, *World Literature Today*, *Journal of Inter-American Studies*, *Latin American Research Review*, *The Latin American Studies Association (LASA)*, *Journal of Black Studies*, *Caribbean Today*, *Central American and Caribbean Affairs*, *A History of Literature in Caribbean*, *Journal of Commonwealth Literature*, *Journal of West Indian Literature*, *Journal of Caribbean Studies*, *Theory, Culture and Society*, *Latin American Research Review*, *Antiquity*, *Latin American Research Today*, and *Explorations in Ethnic Studies*, while Conferences include Caribbean Crossings Conference, Caribbean 2000/Caribe 2000, Caribbean Literary Studies Conference, Caribbean Women Writers and Scholars Conference, West Indian Literature Conference, Caribbean Studies Association, Association of Caribbean Studies Conference, and International Conference on Caribbean Literature. Organizations and References include The Research Institute for the Study of Man (RISM), LANIC Newsroom: Conferences & Events Archive, lanic.utexas.edu/info/ newsroom/conferences/confarc.html, Caribbean Studies Association (CSA), www.gse. harvard.edu/~views/ conferences.html, The Center for Latino, Latin American, and Caribbean Studies (CELAC), Latin American Studies Association, Caribbean Studies Program, Society For Caribbean Studies (U.K.), West Indian Literature, http://www. westindiesbooks.com, Russ Filman's Caribbean Literature, http://www. freenet.hamilton.on.ca/~aa462/cariblit.html, Caribbean Literature Research Web, http://caribnet. upra.edu, and Brown University's Caribbean Literature, http://www.scholars.nus.edu.sg/ landow/post/caribbean/caribov.html

# Notes

1. (ICLC) International Christian Leadership Connections
2. (ACEA) African and Caribbean Evangelical Alliance
3. (CN) Connections Network
4. (FGF) Full Gospel Fellowship

# Works Cited

Achebe, Chinua. *Morning Yet on Creation Day: Essays*. London: Heinemann, 1975.

——."An Image of Africa: Racism in Conrad's *Heart of Darkness*." *Heart of Darkness*. By Joseph Conrad. Ed. Robert Kimbrough. New York: W. W. Norton, 1988. 251-62.

——."Colonialist Criticism." Achebe, *Morning Yet on Creation Day*. 3-18.

Egbaw, Stephen Ekema. "An African Teacher of Conrad's *Heart of Darkness* in America." *Proceedings: The 1993 Conference of the Pennsylvania State Universities*. 1-2 Oct., 1993. Comp. Jim Glimm. Mansfield, PA: Mansfield UP, 1993. 132-41.

Alcorn, Randy. *Money, Possessions and Eternity*. Wheaton: Tyndale House, 1989.

Alexander, Simone A. James. *Mother Imagery: In the Novels of Afro-Caribbean Women*. St. Louis: University of Missouri Press, 2001. http: //www.findarticles.com/cf_dls/m2838/1_37/100959613/p1/article.jhtml

Allis, Jeannette B. "West Indian Literature: A Case for Regional Criticism." Eds. Roberta Knowles and Erika Smilowitz. *Critical Approaches to West Indian Literature*. St. Thomas: College of the Virgin Islands and UWI, 1981. 23-40.

Altbach, Philip G. "Education and Neocolonialism." Ashcroft, *Post-colonial Studies*, 452-56.

Anderson, Paula Grace. "Jean Rhys' *Wide Sargasso Sea*: The Other Side/Both Sides Now." Knowles 237-59.

Angier, Carole. *Jean Rhys: Life and Work*. London: Andre Deutsch, 1990.

Anthony, Michael. *The Year in San Fernando*. London: Deutsch, 1965; Portsmouth, New Hampshire, Heinemann, 1996.

——. *The Games Were Coming*. London, Deutsch, 1963; Boston, Houghton Mifflin, 1968.

——. *Green Days by the River*. Boston, Houghton Mifflin, and London, Deutsch, 1967.

Asante, Molefi Kete. *The Afrocentric Idea*. Philadelphia: Temple UP, 1987.

——. *Afrocentricity*. Trenton: Africa World Press, 1988.

Ashcroft, Bill, Gareth Griffiths, and Helen Tiffin, eds. *The Post-colonial Studies Reader*. New York: Routledge, 1995.

——. *The Empire Writes Back*. London: Routledge, 1989.

*A Child's First Gift: Names for Baby*. Philadelphia: Wyeth-Ayerst Laboratories, 1993.

Barna, George. *The Second Coming of the Church*. New York: Word Publishing, 1998.

Bascom, Harold. *Apata*. New York: Heinemann, 1987.

Baugh, Edward. "Since 1960: Some Highlights." King 78–94.

Beckmann, Susan. "Language as Cultural Identity." *Language and Literature in Multicultural Contexts.* Ed. Satendra Nandan. Suva, Fiji: University of South Pacific, 1983. 66–78.

Bell, D. *Faces at the Bottom of the Well.* New York: Basic Books, 1992.

Bennett, Louise. "Colonization in Reverse." 1966. http://en.wikipedia.org/wiki/ Louise_ Bennett

Bhabha, Homi K. "Representation and the Colonial Text: Critical Exploration of Some Forms of Mimeticism." *The Theory of Reading.* Ed. Frank Gloversmith. Brighton, England: Harvester Press, 1984. 119–20.

——. "Of Mimicry and Men: The Ambivalence of Colonial Discourse." *October* 28 (1984): 125–33.

Bhatnagar, O. P. "Commonwealth Literature: Genesis and Bearings." Eds. G. S. Amur, V. R. N. Prasad, B. V. Nermode, and N. K. Nihalani. *Indian Readings in Commonwealth Literature.* New Delhi: Sterling, 1985. 26–37.

Bloom, Allan. *The Closing of the American Mind: How Higher Education Has Failed Democracy and Impoverished the Souls of Today's Students.* New York: Simon & Schuster, 1987.

Boehmer, Elleke. *Colonial and Postcolonial Literature: Migrant Metaphors.* Oxford: Oxford UP, 1995.

Boxill, Anthony. "Wilson Harris." *Fifty Caribbean Writers.* Ed. Daryl Cumber Dance. London: Greenwood Press, 1986. 187–97.

Brathwaite, Edward Kamau. "Caliban, Ariel, and Unprospero in the Conflict of Creolization: A Study of the Slave Revolt in Jamaica in 1831–32." *Comparative Perspectives on Slavery in the New World Plantation Societies.* Ed. Vera Rubin and Arthur Tuden. New York: New York Academy of Sciences, 1977. 41–62.

——. *Roots.* 1986. Ann Arbor: University of Michigan Press, 1993.

——. *The Arrivants: A New World Trilogy.* 1967. Oxford: Oxford UP, 1973.

——. "The African Presence in the Caribbean."

——. *History of the Voice.*

Brontë, Charlotte. *Jane Eyre.* New York: Knopf, 1960.

Bulhan, Hussein Abdilahi. *Frantz Fanon and the Psychology of Oppression.* New York: Plenum Press, 1985.

Buchan, John. *Prester John.* New York: Houghton, 1910.

Cairns, A. C. *Prelude to Imperialism.* London: Oxford UP, 1965.

Carson, Clayborne. "Biography of Marin Luther King Jr." http: //www.stanford.edu/ group/King/

Carter, Martin. *Poems of Succession.* London: New Beacon Books, 1977.

Caute, David. *Frantz Fanon.* New York: Viking, 1970.

Césaire, Aimé. *Les Armes Miraculeuses (Et les chiens se taisaient).* Paris: Gallimard, 1964.

Cliff, Michelle. *No Telephone to Heaven.* New York: 1987. Plume, 1996.

——. *Abeng.* New York: Penguin, 1985.

Conrad, Joseph. *Heart of Darkness.* 1902. New York: Dover, 1990.

Cox, T. *Cultural Diversity in Organizations: Theory, Research, & Practice.* San Francisco: Berrett-Koehler Publishers, 1993.

Curtin, P. *The Image of Africa.* New York: Macmillan, 1965.

—— *Abeng.* New York: Penguin, 1985.

D'Costa, Jean. "Expression and Communication: Literary Challenges to the Caribbean Polydialectal Writers." *The Journal of Commonwealth Literature* 19.1 (1984): 123–41.

——. "The West Indian Novelist and Language: A Search for a Literary Medium." *Studies in Caribbean Language*. Ed. Alice Carrington. St. Augustine, Trinidad: U West Indies P, 1983. 252-70.

Dabydeen, David. *The Intended*. London: Secker and Warburg, 1991.

Dakes, Fenis Jennings. *Dakes Annotated Reference Bible*. Lawrenceville, GA: Dake Bible Sales, Inc., 1961.

Dance, Daryl Cumber, ed. *Fifty Caribbean Writers*. London: Greenwood Press, 1986.

——. Introduction. Dance 1-8Dash, J. Michael. *Edouard Glissant*. New York: Cambridge University Press, 1995.

Daume, Daphne, ed. *1993 Britannica Book of the Year*. Chicago: Encyclopaedia Britannica, 1993.

Davis, S. "Christianity, Philosophy, and Multiculturalism." *Christian Scholar's Review* XXV.4 (June 1996): 394-408.

Davison, R. B. *West Indian Migrants*. London: Oxford UP, 1962.

Deena, Seodial Frank. "The Irrationality of Bigger Thomas' World: A Frightening View for the Twenty-First Century Urban Population." *College Language Association Journal* 38.1 (Sept. 1994): 20-30.

——. "Colonial and Canonical Control over Third World Writers." *Commonwealth Review* 7.2 (1995-95): 78-111.

——. *Colonization, Canonization, Decolonization, Counter-Canonization: A Comparative Study of Political and Critical Works by Minority Writers*. New York: Peter Lang, 2001.

Dell'Olio, A. "Multiculuralism and Religious Diversity: A Christian Perspective." *Christian Scholar's Review* XXV.4 (June 1996): 459-477.

DeSouza, Dinesh. *Illiberal Education: The Politics of Race and Sex on Campus*. New York: Vintage Books, 1992.

——. *The End of Racism*. New York: The Free Press, 1995.

DeYoung, C. P. *Coming Together: The Bible's Message in an Age of Diversity*. Valley Forge, PA: Judson Press, 1995.

——. *Reconciliation: Our Greatest Challenge-Our Only Hope*. Valley Forge, PA: Judson Press, 1997.

Dhareshwar, Vivek. "Self-fashioning, Colonial Habitus, and Double Exclusion: V. S. Naipaul's *The Mimic Men*." *Criticism* 31.1 (Winter 1989): 75-102.

Donne, John. *Devotions upon Emergent Occasions* (1624) http: //www.island-of-freedom.com/DONNE.HTM

Douglass, Frederick. *Narrative of the Life of Frederick Douglass: An American Slave*. London: Harvard UP, 1960.

DuBois, W. E. B. *The Souls of Black Folk: Essays and Sketches*. New York: The Blue Heron Press, 1953.

Eliot, T. S. "Hollow Men." Kermode 490-94.

——. "The Love Song of J. Alfred Prufrock." Kermode 463-68.

Emery, Mary Lou. *Jean Rhys at "World's End: " Novels of Colonial and Sexual Exile*. Austin: University of Texas Press, 1990.

Erapu, Laban. Introduction. *Miguel Street*. By V. S. Naipaul. London: Heinemann, 1974. xi-xxi.

Evans, T. *Let's Get To Know Each Other: What White Christians Should Know About Black Christians*. Nashville, TN: Thomas Nelson Publishers, 1995.

Fabre, Michael. "Samuel Selvon." *West Indian Literature*. Ed. Bruce King. London: Macmillan, 1979. 111-25.

Fanon, Frantz. *Black Skin White Masks*. Trans. Charles Lam Markmann. New York: Grove Press, 1967.

——. Introduction. *Black Skin White Masks*. Trans. Charles Lam Markmann. New York: Grove Press, 1967. 7-14.

——. *The Wretched of the Earth*. 1966. Trans. Constance Farrington. New York: Grove Press, 1963.

Feagin, J. & Vera, H. *White Racism: The Basics*. New York: Routledge, 1995.

Fong, B. "A View From the Inside: Reflections of a Christian Multiculturalist." *Christian Scholar's Review* XXV.4 (June 1996): 409-20.

Forster, E. M. *A Passage to India*. London: Harcourt, 1924.

Friedman, Ellen G. "Breaking the Master Narrative: Jean Rhys' *Wide Sargasso Sea*." *Breaking the Sequence*. Eds. Ellen G. Friedman and Miriam Fuchs. Princeton: Princeton UP, 1989. 117-28.

Freire, Paulo. *Pedagogy of the Oppressed*. Trans. Myra Bergman Ramos. New York: Continuum, 1990.

Gaede, S. D. *When Tolerance Is No Virtue*. Downer's Grove, IL: InterVarsity Press, 1993.

Gaster, Snally. " Derek W alcott." (http://www.math.buffalo.edu/~sww/peotry/walcottderek. html)

Geneva College. *Blueprint for Diversity*. 1998.

Gikandi, Simon. *Reading Chinua Achebe: Language and Ideology in Fiction*. Nairobi: Heinemann, 1991.

——. "Chinua Achebe and the Post-Colonial Esthetic: Writing, Identity, and National Formation." *Studies in Twentieth Century Literature* 15.1

Gilkes, Michael. *Couvade: A Dream-Play of Guyana*. London: Longman Caribbean, 1974; Dangaroo, 1990.

Glissant, Edouard, and A. J. Arnold, eds. *Caribbean Discourse*. Trans. Michael J. Dash. Charlottesville: University of Virginia Press, 1994.

Gopal, Sarvepalli. *Jawaharlal Nehru: A Biography. Vol. One 1889-1947*. Cambridge: Harvard UP, 1976.

Gosine, Mahin. "Sojourner to Settler: An Introduction." http: //saxakali.com/indocarib/ introduction.htm

Griffiths, Gareth. *A Double Exile: Africa and West Indian Writing Between Two Cultures*. London: Marian Boyars, 1978.

Groden, Michael, and Martin Kreiswirth. eds. *The John Hopkins Guide to Literary Theory and Criticism*. Baltimore: The John Hopkins UP, 1994.

——. "Postcolonial Cultural Studies." Groden 581-84.

Gugelberger, Georg. "Decolonizing the Canon: Considerations of the Third World." *New Literary History: A Journal of Theory and Interpretation* 22.3 (Summer 1991): 505-24.

——. "Postcolonial Cultural Studies." Groden 581-84.

Hacker, A. *Two Nations: Black and White, Separate, Hostile, Unequal*. New York:Charles Scribner's Sons, 1992.

Hamner, Robert D. "Aspects of National Character: V. S. Naipaul and Derek Walcott." Ed. Satendra Nandan. *Language and Literature in Multicultural Contexts*. Suva, Fiji: University of South Pacific, 1983. 179-88.

——. ed. *Critical Perspectives on V. S. Naipaul*. Washington: Three Continents press, 1977.

Harris, Wilson. "The Fabric of the Imagination." Ed. Anna Rutherford. *From Commonwealth to Post-Colonial*. Sydney: Dangaroo Press, 1992. 18-29.

——. *The Womb of Space: The Cross-Cultural Imagination.* Westport, Conn.: Greenwood Press, 1983.

——. *The Palace of the Peacock.* London: Faber, 1960.

——. Harris, Wilson. *Explorations: A Selection of Talks and Articles, 1966-1981.* Mundelstrup, Denmark: Dangaroo Press, 1981.

——. *The Far Journey of Oudin.* London: Faber, 1961.

——. *Heartland.* London: Faber, 1964.

——. *The Whole Armour.* London: Faber, 1962.

——. *The Secret Ladder.* London: Faber, 1963.

——. Harris, Wilson. *Tradition, the Writer and Society: Critical Essays.* London: New Beacon, 1967.

Hassan, Dolly Zulakha. *V. S. Naipaul and the West Indies.* New York: Peter Lang, 1989.

Hathaway, Heather. "Review of Caroline Rody's *The Daughter's Return: African-American and Caribbean Women's Fictions of History.*" New York: Oxford UP, 2001. *African American Review.* Spring, 2003. http://webpub.

Hirsch, E. D. *Cultural Literacy: What Every American Needs to Know.* Boston: Houghton Mifflin, 1987. Revised as *The New Dictionary of Cultural Literacy: What Every American Needs to Know.* Boston: Houghton Mifflin, 2004.

Holy Bible. *Authorized King James Version.* Grand Rapids, MI: Zondervan Bible Publishers, 1983.

Hopkins, A. J. and Peter Cain *European Imperialism: Crisis and Deconstruction, 1914-1990.* London: Longman, 1993.

——. *British Imperialism: Innovation and Expansion, 1688-1914.* London: Longman, 1993.

Howells, Coral Ann. *Jean Rhys.* New York: St. Martin's Press, 1991.

Hume, David. *The Philosophical Works.* 1882. Darmstadt, Germany: Scientia Verlag Aalen, 1964. allegheny.edu/group/LAS/ LatinAmIssues/Articles/Vol13/LAI_vol_13_section _IV.html

Joseph, Margaret Paul. *Caliban in Exile: The Outsider in Caribbean Fiction* NewYork: Greenwood Press, 1992.

John, Errol. *Moon on a Rainbow Shawl.* London: Faber, 1958.

Kallen, H. M. *Culture and Democracy in the United States.* New York: Boni and Liveright, 1924.

——. *Cultural Pluralism and the American Idea.* Philadelphia: University of Pennsylvania Press, 1956.

Katzinski, Vera M. "Caribbean Theory and Criticism." Groden 138-42.

Kehrein, Glen and Raleigh Washington. *Breaking Down Walls: A Model for Reconciliation in an Age of Racial Strife.* Chicago: Moody Press, 1993.

Khan, Ismith. "Dialect in West Indian Literature." Ed. Lloyd Brown. *The Black Writer in Africa and the Americas.* Los Angeles: Hennessey and Ingalls, 1973. 141-64.

Killam, G. D. *Africa in English Fiction 1874-1939.* Lagos: Ibadan UP, 1968.

——. Introduction. *An Introduction to the Writings of Ngég«.* By Killam. London: Heinemann, 1980. 1-19.

Kincaid, Jamaica. *Annie John.* New York: New American Library, 1986.

——. *At the Bottom of the River.* New York: Plume, 1992.

——. *The Autobiography of My Mother.* New York: Farrar, Straus, Giroux, 1996.

——. *Lucy.* New York: Farrar, Straus, Giroux, 1990.

——. *My Brother.* New York: Farrar, Straus, Giroux, 1997.

——. *A Small Place.* New York: Farrar, Straus, Giroux, 1988.

King, Bruce. Ed. *West Indian Literature*. Hamden, CT: Archon Books, 1979.

——. *V. S. Naipaul*. New York: St. Martin's Press, 1993.

King, Florence. *Southern Ladies and Gentlemen*. New York: Stein and Day, 1975.

King, Martin Luther, Jr. "I Have a Dream Speech." http://www.usconstitution.net/dream.html

Kipling, Rudyard. *The Man Who Would Be King*. London: A H Wheeler & Co of Allahabad, 1888.

Kirpal, Viney. *The Third World Novel of Expatriation: A Study of Emigre Fiction by Indian, West African and Caribbean Writers*. New Delhi: Sterling, 1989.

Knowles, Roberta, and Erika Smilowitz, eds. *Critical Approaches to West Indian Literature*. St. Thomas, US Virgin Islands: College of the Virgin Islands and UWI, 1981.

Kraze, Frieda. *Heim Neuland*. Frankfurt: Stuttgart and Leipzig, 1909.

Lamming, George. *In The Castle of My Skin*. New York: McGraw, 1953; Ann Arbor: U of Michigan P, 2005.

——. Introduction. *In The Castle of My Skin*. New York: McGraw, 1953; Ann Arbor: U of Michigan P, 2005. xxxv-xlvi.

——. *The Pleasures of Exile*. Ann Arbor: U of Michigan P, 1992.

——. *Natives of My Person*. London: Longman Caribbean, 1972.

Lapping, Brian. *End of Empire*. New York: ST. Martin's Press, 1985.

Le Gallez, Paula. *The Rhys Woman*. New York: St. Martin's Press, 1990.

Loomba, Ania. *Colonialism/Postcolonialism*. New York: Routledge, 1998.

Louis, Wm. Roger. Editor-in-chief. *The Oxford History of the British Empire*. Oxford: Oxford University Press, 1998-2000.

Lovelace, Earl. *While Gods Are Falling*. New York: Collins, 1965.

——. *The Schoolmaster*. New York: Collins, 1968.

——. *The Dragon Can't Dance*. London: André Deutsch, 1979.

——. *The Wine of Astonishment*. London: André Deutsch, 1982.

——. *Jestina's Calypso and Other Plays*. Heinemann, 1984

——. *A Brief Conversion and Other Stories* Heinemann, 1988

——. *Salt* Faber and Faber, 1996

Luthy, Herbert. "Colonization and the Making of Mankind." Mazlish 26-37.

Lyn, Gloria. "'A Thing Called Art': V. S. Naipaul's *The Mimic Men*." Knowles 53-70.

MacDonald, Bruce. "Symbolic Action in Three of V. S. Naipauls Novels." Hammer 242-64.

Maes-Jelinek, Hena. "Wilson Harris." *International Literature in English: Major Essays on Major Writers*. Ed. Robert Ross. New York: Garland Publishing, 1991. 447-59.

Mannoni, Octave. *Prospero and Caliban: The Psychology of Colonialism*. 1964. Trans. Pamela Powerland. New York: Frederick A.Praeger, 1956.

Mason, Philip. Foreword. *Prospero and Caliban: The Psychology of Colonialism*. By O. Mannoni. New York: Praeger, 1956. 9-15.

——. *Prospero's Magic: Some Thoughts on Class and Race*. London: Oxford UP, 1962.

Matuz, Roger. "Multiculturalism in Literature and Education." *Contemporary Literary Criticism*. Ed. Roger Matuz. Vol. 70. Detroit: Gale, 1992. 361-62.

McArthur, John. Electronic Bible Commentary. 2007.

Memmi, Albert. *The Colonizer and the Colonized*. 1967. Trans. Howard Greenfield. Boston: Beacon Press, 1965.

Miller, J. *The Unmaking of Americans: How Multiculturalism Has Undermined America's Assimilation Ethic*. New York: The Free Press, 1998.

Miller, Karl. "V. S. Naipaul and the New Order." Hammer 111-25.

Mittelholzer, Edgar. *Corentyne Thunder*. London: Eyre and Spottiswoode, 1941.

——. *A Morning at the Office*. London: Hogarth Press, 1950.

——. *Children of Kaywana*. London: Peter Neville, 1952.

——. *Kaywana Stock: The Harrowing of Hubertus*. London: Secker and Warburg, 1954.

——. *Kaywana Blood*. London: Secker and Warburg, 1958.

——. *My Bones and My Flute*. London: Secker and Warburg, 1955.

——. *A Swarthy Boy (autobiography)*. London: Putnam, 1963.

Mohabir, Philip. *Building Bridges*. London: Hodder and Stoughton, 1988.

——. *Pioneers or Settlers*. London: Hodder and Stoughton, 1990.

——. *Worlds Within Reach: Cross-cultural Witness*. London: Hodder and Stoughton, 1993.

——. *Hands of Jesus*. London: Hodder and Stoughton, 2003.

——. Messages and Letters.

——. Interviews.

Moore-Gilbert, Bart. *Postcolonial Theory: Contexts, Practices, Politics*. London: Verso, 1997.

Moresco, Emanuel. *Colonial Questions and Peace*. Paris: International Institute of Intellectual Co-operation, 1939.

——. "Wilson Harris." King 179-95.

Morris, Mervyn. Introduction. *Old Story Time*. By Trevor Rhone. London: Longman, 1981. v-xiv.

Morris, Robert K. *Paradoxes of Order: Some Perspectives on the Fiction of V. S. Naipaul*. Columbia: UP of Missouri, 1975.

Mott, Stephen Charles. *Biblical Ethics and Social Change*. New York: Oxford UP, 1982.

MSNBC. "Mother Teresa, in her Own Words." Internet. 1-3.

Munger, Robert. Electronic Bible Commentary. 2007.

Nadel, George H., and Perry Curtis. Introduction. *Imperialism and Colonialism*. Bruce Mazlish. Ed. New York: Macmillan, 1964. 1-26.

Naipaul, V. S. *Miguel Street*. London: Heinemann, 1974.

——. *A Bend in the River*. New York: Knopf, 1979.

——. *An Area of Darkness*. London: Penguin Books, 1968.

——. *The Mimic Men*. New York: Penguin Books, 1969.

——. *The Middle Passage*. London: Deutsch, 1962.

——. *The Mystic Masseur*. New York: Knopf, 1982.

——. *The Enigma of Arrival*. New York: Knopf, 1987.

——. "V. S. Naipaul—Nobel Lecture: Two Worlds." http://www.nobel.se/literature/laureates/2001/naipaul-lecture-e.html

Nazareth, Peter. "*The Mimic Men* as a Study of Corruption." *An African View of Literature*. By Nazareth. Evanston: Northwestern UP, 1974. 76-93.

Nightingale Peggy. "V. S. Naipaul: Finding the Present in the Past." *International Literature in English: Major Essays on Major Writers*. Ed. Robert L. Ross. New York: Garland Publishing, 1991. 525-34.

Ngugi, James. *Homecoming: Essays on African and Caribbean Literature, Culture and Politics*. London: Heinemann, 1972.

Olaussen, Maria. "Jean Rhys' Construction of Blackness as Escape from White Femininity in *Wide Sargasso Sea*." *ARIEL* 24.2 (April 1993): 65-82.

Orme, Steve. "Review of *Moon on a Rainbow Shawl*: Eclipse Theatre at Nottingham Playhouse." http://www.britishtheatreguide.info/reviews/rainbowshawl-rev.htm

Palmer, Colin A. *The First Passage: Blacks in the Americas, 1502–1617.* New York: Oxford UP, 1995.

Palmer, P. J. *The Courage to Teach: Exploring the Inner Landscape of a Teacher's Life.* San Francisco: Jossey-Bass Publishers, 1998.

Paquet, Sandra Pouchet. Foreword. Lamming, *Pleasures.* vii–xxvii.

Perkins, John. *Beyond Charity: The Call to Christian Community Development.* Grand Rapids: Baker Books, 1993.

Raiskin, Judith L. *Snow on the Cane Fields: Women's Writing and Creole Subjectivity.*

Ramchand, Kenneth. "Aborigines: Their Role in West Indian Literature." *Jamaica Journal* 3.4 (Dec. 1969): 51–54.

——. *The West Indian Novel and Its Background.* London: Faber and Faber, 1970.

——. Introduction. *The Lonely Londoners.* By Samuel Selvon. London: Wingate, 1956. 3-21.

Ramraj, Victor. "The All-Embracing Christlike Vision: Tone and Attitude in *The Mimic Men.*" Hammer 127-36.

Reid, V. S. *Sixty Five.* London: Longman, 1960.

Ridley, Hugh. *Images of Imperial Rule.* New York: ST. Martin Press, 1983.

Rhone, Trevor. *Old Story Time.* London: Longman, 1981.

——. Personal Interview. March 1998.

Rhys, Jean. *Wide Sargasso Sea.* New York: W. W. Norton, 1982.

Robinson, Ronald Edward and John Gallagher. *Africa and the Victorians: The Official Mind of Imperialism.* London: Macmillan, 1961.

Rodney, Walter. *How Europe Underdeveloped Africa.* Washington: Howard UP, 1974. Minneapolis: University of Minnesota Press, 1996.

Rody, Caroline. *The Daughter's Return: African–American and Caribbean Women's Fictions of History.* New York: Oxford UP, 2001.

Rohlehr, Gordon. 'The Ironic Approach." *West Indian Literature.* London: Mac Millan Press, 1979.

——. "The Ironic Approach: The Novels of V. S. Naipaul." Hammer 178-93.

Rushdie, Salman. *Imaginary Homelands: Essays and Criticism, 1981-1991.* London: Penguin Books, 1992.

Said, Edward W. *Orientalism.* New York: Vintage, 1979.

Seenarine, Moses. Foreword. http://saxakali.com/indocarib/sojourner1f.htm

Selvon, Samuel. *The Lonely Londoners.* London: Wingate, 1956.

——. *A Brighter Sun.* London: Longman, 1952.

——. *Moses Ascending.* London: Davis-Poynter, 1975.

——. *Moses Migrating.* London: Longman, 1983.

Shakespeare, William. *The Tempest. The Unabridged William Shakespeare.* Ed. William George Clark and William Aldis Wright. Philadelphia: Running Press, 1989. 1-26.

Spivak, Gayatri Chakravorty. *A Critique of Postcolonial Reason: Toward A History of the Vanishing Present.* Cambridge: Harvard UP, 1999.

Soyinka, Wole. *The Lion and The Jewel.* London: Oxford UP, 1962.

Sproul, R. C. *Ethics and the Christian: Right and Wrong in Today's World.* Wheaton, IL: Tyndale, 1989.

Staley, Thomas F. *Jean Rhys: A Critical Study.* Austin: University of Texas Press, 1979.

Street, Brian V. *The Savage in Literature: Representations of 'Primitive' Society in English Fiction 1858-1920.* London: Routledge and Keegan Paul, 1975.

——. "The Muse of History." Ashcroft 370-74.

———. "The Nobel Lecture: The Antilles: Fragments of Epic Memory." *The New Republic* 28 Dec. 1992: 26-32.

*The Bible: Authorized King James Version.* Grand Rapids, MI: Zondervan Bible Publishers, 1983.

*The Bible.* Lawrenceville: Dake Bible Sales, Inc., 1961.

Thomas, Dylan. "Do Not Go Gentle into that Good Night." http://www.bigeye.com/donotgo.htm

Thompson, Frand Charles, ed. *The Thompson Chain-Reference Bible: New International Version.* Grand Rapids: Zondervan, 1983.

Wagnew, Peter. *Church Growth and the Whole Gospel: A Biblical Mandate.* San Francisco: Harper, 1981.

Walcott, Derek. *Another Life.* London: Cape, 1973.

———. *Ti-Jean and His Brothers.* New York: Farrar, 1972.

———. "What the Twilight Says: An Overture." *Dream on Monkey Mountain and Other Plays.* By Walcott. New York: Farrar, 1970. 3-40.

———. "The Muse of History." Ashcroft 370-74.

———. "The Nobel Lecture: The Antilles: Fragments of Epic Memory." *The New Republic* 28 Dec. 1992: 26-32. (http://www.kirjasto.sci.fi/walcott.htm).

———. *Selected Poems.* New York: Farrar, 1964.

———. "A Far Cry From Africa. *Derek Walcott Collected Poems 1948-84.* New York: Farrar, 1986. 17-18.

———. "The Muse of History." *Is Massa Day Dead? Black Moods in the Caribbean.* Ed. Orde Combs. New York: Anchor Books, 1974. 1-28. Also at:

———. "The Muse of History." *Critics on Caribbean Literature: Readings in Literary Criticism.* Edward Baugh. Ed. New York: St. Martin's Press, 1978. 38-43. http://www.rism.org/lcr/at_the_LCR/literature/walcott/walcott_sites.html

wa Thiong'o, Ngũgĩ. *Barrel of a Pen: Resistance to Repression in Neo-Colonial Kenya.* London: Heinemann, 1983.

———. *Decolonising the Mind: The Politics of Language in African Literature.* London: James Currey, 1986.

Wilentz, Gay. "English Is a Foreign Anguish: Caribbean Writers and the Disruption of the Colonial Canon." *Decolonizing Tradition: New Views of Twentieth-Century 'British' Literary Canons.* Ed. Karen R. Lawrence. Urbana: U Illinois P, 1992. 261-78.

White, Landeg. *V. S. Naipaul: A Critical Introduction.* New York: Harper, 1975.

Wright, Richard. *Native Son.* 1940. New York: Harper Perennial, 1993.

———. *Uncle Tom's Children.* New York: HarperPerenial, 1993.

———. *American Hunger.* New York: Harper, 1977.

———. *Black Boy.* New York: Harper, 1945.

# Index

*Caribbean Studies* treats all aspects of Caribbean culture and society, including, but not necessarily limited to, literatures, history, film, music, art, geography, politics, languages, and social sciences. Studies may focus on European, Amerindian, African, or Asian heritages or on a combination of any/all of the above. Linear and chronological approaches, as well as comparative studies are welcome. Places and/or cultures under study may include English-, Spanish-, French-, or Dutch-speaking areas in any time frame or discipline. Manuscripts may be written in English, Spanish, or French, preferably in the language in which the author feels most comfortable. Studies may be on contemporary or previous periods and, if appropriate, can draw comparisons with other global regions.

For additional information about the series or for the submission of manuscripts, please contact:

Tamara Alvarez-Detrell and Michael G. Paulson
General Editors
c/o Dr. Heidi Burns
Peter Lang Publishing, Inc.
P.O. Box 1246
Bel Air, MD 21014-1246

To order other books in this series, please contact our Customer Service Department:

800-770-LANG (within the U.S.)
(212) 647-7706 (outside the U.S.)
(212) 647-7707 FAX

Or browse online by series at:

www.peterlang.com